SPIRITOLOGY

SPIRITOLOGY

Your Secret Guide to Breaking Your Religious Shackles &
Becoming Spiritually Sovereign

Mastering & Manifesting Your Promised Land Within

(From a Prophetic View)

PHYLLIS Y. WHITLEY

Printed in the United States

Published by Phyllis Y. Whitley 12/11/2020
Self-Whisper LLC
www.selfwhisper.com
www.whispervise.org

ISBN: 979-8-9879970-0-0

Disclaimer: *The topics, information, spiritual and mental advice presented in this book is based on training, personal experience, and research. Readers are encouraged to seek the counsel of competent professionals with regard to such matters. The author of this book does not dispense medical or professional advice as a form of treatment or healing from internal or external wounds without the advice of an attending professional physician, licensed therapist, or spiritual leader either directly or indirectly. All of the recommendations and considerations herein contained are made without guarantee on the part of the author or the publisher, their agents, counterparts, or employees. The author and publisher disclaim all liability in connection with the use of information presented herein.*

Because of the Internet's dynamic nature, any web addresses or links contained in this book may have changed since publication and may no longer be valid.

DEDICATION

To God, my Friend & Infinite Father
To my deceased mother, an angel at work now.
To my daughter, a virtuous princess, Priscilla. To my
WhisperVise Prophetic Prayer Warriors (WPPW) for
praying my book into existence.

Table of Contents

Acknowledgments

To my Divine Father, God, who showed me the difference between religion and righteousness while blessing me with a platform to illustrate His true image.

To my daughter Priscilla, when the nurse first brought you to my bedside in the delivery ward of the hospital, God spoke to me and said, "she will be a blessing to you in ways you will never believe." I chuckled and thought to myself, "how can my child be that much of a blessing to me." Well, today, she continues to bless me with her patience, grace, respect, beautiful personality, faith, high Godly standards, good morals, and unconditional love each day. God was right!

To my late mother Dorothy M. Daniels (1934-2018), who showed me what unconditional love was and what a true wonder woman is.

To my late Sister Sylvia L. Hawes (1959-2001), who spoke to my spirit for me not to cry for her absence because it was just an illusion.

To a special friend, J. F., who God used mightily to walk me through one of my darkest hours, my mother's death.

To the late Christina White, who was an example of how a real queen is supposed to treat her king.

To Archbishop E. Bernard Jordan and Pastor Prophetess Debra Jordan, who are the founders of the school of the prophets (P.O.M.E.), where I awakened my prophetic gifts of prophecy.

To all my enemies and limitations, thank you for being my stepping-stone to success.

To all my veteran and current Self-Whisper clients who believed in my gifts before I did and allowed my transparency to wake up their infinite being.

To all my good spiritual leaders and coaches who pushed me off my wilderness cliff, knowing I would become a truly virtuous woman.

To all my false and fake spiritual leaders that taught me what not to be and have provided me a basis for the topic of this book. Bless you!

Introduction

Revealing the Science of Spiritual Slaughter Within the Church

"And you shall know the truth, and the truth shall make you free."

John 8:32 (NKJV)

Living across many states, I was fortunate enough to become a member of churches of various denominations. It was at these churches that I experienced seven hurt cycles. It shocked me that I would have to experience such hurts from devoted church-going people. Churches are full of holy people with high statuses that form cliques around the pastor. They work to keep gifted individuals out, making them feel like outsiders because they feel spiritually threatened and replaceable. This has been a common theme I experienced at most churches I have joined. The seven cycles I have experienced or witnessed are judgment, rejection, promiscuity, backstabbing, greed, competition, and secrecy, especially from the leader and their downline clique leaders.

I spent years asking myself some of the same questions over and over. Why am I not attracting my life desires? Why are religious people still suffering while atheists are prospering every day? Why do church members and leaders who attend church several times a week cannot pay their bills while a non-church person is blessed with their dream job and a six-figure salary? Why are prophets and prayer warriors not seeing the answers to their prayers, but their non-praying neighbors live their dream and are happy? How long does a person have to fast before they see a breakthrough?

Why are many virgins and celibate women believing in a spouse remain single past their childbearing years while many sexually active women are found by their husbands in their youth? Why are men with a king's heart overlooked or used by women who want a bad boy? Why are so many of God's people who pay tithes are living from paycheck to paycheck while non-tithers are enjoying trips around the world as they steadily climb their successful ladder? How has the church become like a multi-billion-dollar business industry? The list of questions could still go on.

After decades of being wrapped around religious dogma and minimizing my self-worth, I became discouraged with the lack of good manifestations in my own life. As I listened to religious leaders preaching and teaching, I was constantly faced with the same religious decrees about how I am expected to wait for God. I am not good enough. The devil is to blame and to make sure I take care of the pastor so that God will take care of me. Soon, I was diagnosed with breast cancer, lacking in my body and mind, and spirit. I began to look at the source of the problems, looking without (external problems) and not looking from within myself (consciousness). I noticed so many Christians and churchgoers suffering from spiritual sickness, from incorrect self-love due to religious traditions and chains. I began opening a path to spiritual awakening, consciousness renewal, self-realization, and mind mastery through my consulting group's development.

Years were spent studying great philosophers' teachings, self-help books, Proverbs, and listening to proven motivational gurus. Relying on my education, counseling, mentorship, coaching skills, personal experiences, and God-given gifts, I began creating spiritual solutions that would reach millions of people. Those who have experienced hurt from the church and are ready to let go of their religious limitations and embrace the true loving God of unlimited possibilities. Get ready to throw away your old religious pain and take back what is rightfully yours! Heaven is here on earth where all your dreams do come true. With over 25 years of proven client success, I am now ready to guide you to breaking your **Religious Shackles (bondage)** and becoming **Spiritually Sovereign (freedom)** – mastering and manifesting your promise land within!

> *"But you are a chosen people, a royal priesthood, a holy nation, God's special possession, that you may declare the praises of him who called you out of darkness into his wonderful light."*

> *1 Peter 2:9 (NIV)*

✇ Chapter 1 ✇

Shackles

(Shackles Song Artist Mary Mary)

"But woe unto you, scribes and Pharisees, hypocrites! for ye shut up the kingdom of heaven against men: for ye neither go in yourselves, neither suffer ye them that are entering to go in."

Matthew 23:13 (KJV)

RELIGIOUS SHACKLES CHALLENGE: THE RISE OF RELIGION BONDAGE

From the 5th century B.C. to the 1st century A.D., there had been waves of various religious sects known as Pharisees, Scribes, Sadducees, and Sanhedrin. These religious sects were well-learned masters in their trade, or field of work, until their encounter with a true master: Jesus Christ. These were religious teachers, priests, scholars, and writers of high authority with the knowledge of everyday societal happenings in their parts of the country, including the increasing popularity of Jesus. The question of the day was how to deal with a man that believed himself equal with God throwing away all religious laws, beliefs, and traditional practices? This is where they began to play their role by enclosing darkness on everything Jesus stood for. However, they failed in understanding that their opponent, Jesus Christ, was more than just flesh and blood. He was also spirit.

His spirit, his divinity – the God part of him, surpassed common religious intelligence. The supernatural miracles he performed were beyond the understanding of religious authority. Their mind was in bondage. Having familiarity with and understanding of bondage, the religious sects sought to put Jesus in bondage. They lied on Jesus, criticized, beat on, spit on, and ultimately hung him from the cross to hold on to their traditional bondage practices – their *Religious Shackles*. Regardless of how the story ends, remember that God was always in control of this biblical play. Every character played a role that must be carried out. Religious authority was fulfilling the role of their father – the devil. However, God's plan overrides the planning and workings of the devil. God's plan went beyond the crucifixion's short-term sufferings and had the devil any inkling of what God had in store, he would have tried to stop the crucifixion. Yes, God is always in control! He has given to those who believe in Him the power to do greater work than even the Master Jesus did because we are a multiplication of him.

> *"Verily, verily, I say unto you, He that believeth on me, the works that I do shall he do also; and greater works than these shall he do; because I go unto my Father."*

> *John 14:12 (KJV)*

SPIRITUAL SOVEREIGNTY SOLUTION: FREEDOM SPELL

> *"The Spirit of the Sovereign LORD is on me because the LORD has anointed me to proclaim good news to the poor. He has sent me to bind up the brokenhearted, to proclaim freedom for the captives and release from darkness for the prisoners."*

> *Isaiah 61:1 (NIV)*

You Are Free

Rejoice! The crucifixion affirmed that Jesus has authority over both heaven and earth. We have been given a choice to believe in our own empowerment to feed his sheep: making disciples of those who also wish to believe by revealing the *Gospel* (good spell) of *Spiritual Sovereignty* (freedom) or revealing the bad spell of *Religious Shackles* (bondage).

God has given us free will to choose this day of life or death by learning how to feed ourselves good news, so our body, mind, and soul are disciplined to carry out God's purpose for us. His purpose is to bestow upon us abundant life. Choosing life is choosing God – being one with Him so that we too shall do greater work. The gospel is a spell of blessings to those who love Him, but those who choose death will attract the deadliest spell of all: called RELIGION.

"I call heaven and earth to record this day against you, that I have set before you, life and death, blessing, and cursing. Therefore, choose life, that both thou and thy seed may live."

Deuteronomy 30:19 (KJV)

Spiritual Sovereignty Action

Put a good spell on yourself!

SELF-WHISPER EXERCISE

1. What spells have you allowed to dictate your life? Religion or Gospel, and why?

2. Are you truly living life to the fullest in spiritual freedom? Or are you being held back by religious rhetoric?

MEDITATION QUOTES

"The beginning of loving God is loving yourself; the creation can't hate the creator."

Phyllis Y Whitley

"I am the master of my fate: I am the captain of my soul."

Nelson Mandela

MEDITATION THERAPY

Today, I let go of religious shackles that kept me in bondage and violated my flesh.

Today, I put on the clothing of Spiritual Sovereignty as I accept a life of freedom.

Today, I believe in the true power of God, and I look within myself to find Him.

Today, I stop the spells of religion and replace it with the Gospel.

Today, I take my power back from false leaders as I connect with my God within.

Today, I soak up the word of God all day long.

Today, I live my life in abundance, humbly.

Today, I am attracting the right people, places, and things to carry out my life's purpose.

Thank you, God, within!

⚘ Chapter 2 ⚘

Battle Scars

(Battle Scars Song Artist Lupe Fiasco & Guy Sebastian)

"For we wrestle not against flesh and blood, but against principalities, against powers, against the rulers of the darkness of this world, against spiritual wickedness in high places."

Ephesians 6:12 (KJV)

RELIGIOUS SHACKLES CHALLENGE: SPIRITUAL WARFARE

Today, religiously shackled churches thrive in putting the focus on the physical being and the sin that comes with it. There is little understanding of why, after so many years of learning religious dogma and attending church every time the doors open, members are still having trouble with truly living out their own salvation. The truth is, they were never taught to know God personally. Research shows that most church members are living a life of bondage, believing that this is God's will, which is actually taking them further away from God. There is no surprise that small churches never grow past their faithful 20 members. At the same time, megachurches serve as a revolving door where every member is just a number to the untouchable spiritual leader.

Sadly, religious-spiritual leaders exist to feed and nurture the spiritual baby inside you to stay as a baby. Their teachings and practices stunt your growth and force you to become dependent on their disillusioned teachings that separate you further from God. As your carnal egotistical desires give rise, soon you will be living a double life – the image of a saint on the outside and a devil within. You will find yourself living life in the wilderness, always searching for God outside of themselves, consistently asking, "Is this really God?" Soon, you find yourself either no longer attending church altogether or giving yourself wholeheartedly to the devil, continuing to broadcast your Christianity publicly while blindly leading those around you to the house of hell called Religion.

You may also do the unthinkable. That is to become a leader so you can have authority over the vulnerable. This is the beginning of Shepherd Slaughter. Alternatively, you may give yourself over to serving, hooking up with the vulnerable until your selfish desires choke and cut your destiny short with God. Religious shackles create religious hypocrites that blind you from the truth. You are left on the spiritual battlefield without the proper instructions from your Highest General – God, that provides the manuscript on winning the spiritual warfare.

"He also shall be my salvation, for an hypocrite could not come before Him."

Job 13:16 (KJV)

SPIRITUAL SOVEREIGNTY SOLUTION: ARMOR OF GOD

"Therefore, put on the full armor of God, so that when the day of evil comes, you may be able to stand your ground, and after you have done everything, to stand."

Ephesians 6:13 (NIV)

Winning

If you did not get the memo that you are at war, let me be the first to tell you that this war is unseen, and the battlefield is in your mind. Yes! It started the minute you set out in your heart to accept Jesus as your Lord and savior. But the religious shackles leaders will not teach you this because they are living in the darkness where they cannot see the light – God.

Remember the religious groups of Jesus's time and how they questioned every miracle he did? Well, they were not in tune with his spiritual self, which was God in action. Since salvation involves the spiritual side of you, those bondage spirits hate you for your divinity too.

Take notice that accepting God into your heart is more than a physical act on your church's stage. It is also a spiritual request that you are ready to become a holistic being with God, giving Him your mind, body, and soul so He can manifest Himself through your highest self. Salvation is an inside job that requires feeding your spirit the right food (thoughts) through His most extraordinary manuscript: the Bible. Because the devil knows that he lost the battle with Jesus at Calvary, the only thing he can do is bring fiery illusions to your mind causing you to live in the wilderness, missing your very own promised land.

Spiritual sovereignty will dress you in God's word by feeding your mind with righteous thoughts, replacing your old seeds of doubt as you consistently walk by faith and not by your five senses but through God. No longer will your mind be idled. His word will teach you to manifest your dreams and desires so that you will be a winner in the game of life. Learn your opponent's tactics so you can stand and not be moved by his illusions:

1. The **truth** of yourself is the belt that holds you up.
2. **Righteousness** is your breastplate protecting your heart.

3. The good news (gospel) of **peace** is your ready fitted feet.
4. **Faith** is your extinguisher, shielding you from the devil's illusion arrows.
5. Disciplining your mind is your helmet of **salvation** and living in **God's word** is your sword of the spirit.

"Stand firm then, with the belt of truth buckled around your waist, with the breastplate of righteousness in place, and with your feet fitted with the readiness that comes from the gospel of peace. In addition to all this, take up the shield of faith, with which you can extinguish all the flaming arrows of the evil one. Take the helmet of salvation and the sword of the Spirit, which is the word of God."

Ephesians 6:14-17 (NIV).

Spiritual Sovereignty Action

Read God's whole manuscript.

SELF-WHISPER EXERCISE

1. Have you read God's manuscript, or do you rely on your spiritual leader to read it?

2. Are you living in a war zone without any instructions?

3. Do you know your opponent's tactics?

Do you know how to use your weapons of warfare?

MEDITATION QUOTES

"Your flesh has one job; to kill you before you realize you have a spirit."

Phyllis Y. Whitley

"The most common way people give up their power is by thinking they don't have any."

Alice Walker

MEDITATION THERAPY

Forgive me as I whisper to myself, the *I Am*, for not mastering my whole self in these areas: my temple, my faith, my wants and desires, my idols, and my worship. Forgive me for believing the lies that You and I are separated; thus, thinking unrighteous and falling short of your Glory.

I now believe and receive that we are one in spirit, and I am saved from lack of_____ through your son Jesus Christ who came to show me how to live abundantly so that my cup can run over unto others. At this moment, I choose life as I promise to use my kingdom keys and Godly talents to increase, multiply, and bring forth good fruits in my season.

I come back to awareness like the prodigal son surrendering my body, mind, and spirit to your higher laws. I consciously will think of good things as you order my footsteps to my promised land as I strive to have inner and outer conversations that are pleasing to your ears in hopes of yielding a good report as you flood my mind with your Holy Spirit to teach and comfort me. I will process the fruits of the spirit daily while embracing an example of kingdom life and leaving an influential legacy for my future generations.

Thank you for being my Lord, my Father, my King, my Truth, and my Higher Self. Amen!

☙ **Chapter 3** ☙

What's Going On?

(What's Going On Song Artist Marvin Gaye)

"Be sober, be vigilant; because your adversary, the devil, as a roaring lion, walketh about, seeking whom he may devour."

1 Peter 5:8

RELIGIOUS SHACKLES CHALLENGE: REBELLIOUS SEEDS

In today's world, those religious shackles live on as rebellious spirits roaming around the earth, duplicating their seeds of rebellion to keep you from finding your true self, your divinity in God. Let us take a sneak preview in history to find the origin of this rebellious spirit, the opposition.

The first rebellious spirit appeared as a serpent causing Adam to rebel against God after receiving orders about the tree of life. You might say, "what about Eve, wasn't she deceived by the serpent?" Yes! But her story did not match what God commanded Adam before her existence, "to eat from any tree in the garden of Eden except the tree of knowledge or he would die" *(Genesis 2)*.

How did the serpent know what God told Adam when the serpent was not named yet? Could this be Lucifer, who was present when God first made heaven and earth? Did Adam forget what God told him? Did Eve forget what her husband told her? Regardless, we know that God's word was doubted. Eve decided to walk by sight, seeing the fruit of that tree delightful to eat. Eve listened to and believed the words of the serpent, which was a *religious shackle* in disguise. She made it her god; likewise, Adam believed Eve making her his god and causing a curse to be put on all three of them – Adam, Eve, and the serpent).

In the Biblical book of Genesis, chapter 1 tells us that everything was formless and empty in the beginning. Creation began with the word, and that word *was* God, who is spirit. God created all things from the invisible: spirit. Since God is spirit and He made man in His image, so too was Adam's spirit. Eve came out from Adam, and he named her. Then they became one spirit. Due to the curse, God drove both Adam and Eve out of his presence *(thought),* leaving them both absent from the garden of Eden *(God's mind)* into what we know of as earth – a physical place.

God clothed Adam and Eve with a physical body called skin because they both became physical human beings the moment Adam ate the fruit, not when Eve ate the fruit. Therefore, they both hid from God at moments noticed that they were naked, or should I say, after they noticed their lack and limitation. This became a ripple effect of a rebellious spirit seeking to embody itself in people for generations to come.

I believe Lucifer was with God initially, so he was the original spirit of rebellion kicked out from Heaven (God's presence or thought). The religious know him as the devil or Satan. Unfortunately, his name is upon their lips more than the name of Jesus, no joke! Regardless of what others told you, the devil is not a red-horned monster, but instead, he is a spirit that brings doubt to your mind, yes! The next time you question God, refrain from saying, "the devil did it!" Try saying, "doubt made me do it." Moreover, if doubt made you do it, then the devil is within anyone that permits it to reside within them.

According to the Urantia Book (53:2.1), Lucifer made Satan his rebellious assistant and the head of fallen angels after being kicked out from Heaven. He then disguised himself as a serpent to deceive Eve, as jealousy in Cain to murder his brother, Abel, as the fraud in Jacob to trick his father Isaac, as complainers in the Israelites who missed the promised land, as disobedience in King Saul that tried to kill David, and as the form of religious shackles in the Pharisees, Scribes, Sadducees, and Sanhedrin who fought against Jesus's divinity. In the end, they all entertained destructive thoughts hindering themselves and future generations to come.

"How you are fallen from heaven, O Lucifer, son of the morning! How you are cut down to the ground, you who weakened the nations!"

Isaiah 14:12 (NKJV)

SPIRITUAL SOVEREIGNTY SOLUTION: REPLACE YOUR ILLUSIONS

"And ye shall know the truth, and the truth shall make you free."

John 8:32 (KJV)

At Last

A spiritually sovereign soul must have truth in their arsenal. The truth will not only set you free from the bondage of religion; it will also guard your mind against the many mind tricks the devil tries to set up for you. He will go through family, friends, and religious leaders with lies because these are the people you trust. Once you believe their lies, it opens the door for the devil seeds to take residence in your mind and rename himself the enemy (he that is in you).

As you allow truth to take up residence within you, the devil will go after your heart. Become righteous and have faith, knowing that God will work abundantly and wonderfully through your mind to manifest accordingly. *"And he believed in the LORD; and he counted it to him for righteousness" (Genesis 15:6).* Remember, every time you believe in the devil's illusions, religious shackles will push you further from God's promises. Instead, you are moving closer to the wilderness of doubt and broken hearts. Now that you know this truth, are you ready to use the power that works in you?

> *"Now to Him who is able to do exceedingly abundantly above all that we ask or think according to the power that works in us."*

> *Ephesians 3:20 (NKJV)*

Spiritual Sovereignty Action

Replace the devil's illusions with God's Truth.

SELF-WHISPER EXERCISE

1. What lies have you believed about yourself?

2. Have you given into the devil's illusions and why?

3. Where have you seen your lack and limitations?

4. What truths can you create for yourself?

MEDITATION QUOTES

"Distractions are a waste of time; excuses are a waste of words."

Phyllis Y. Whitley

"All disease originates in the mind. Nothing appears on the body unless there is a mental pattern corresponding to it."

Joseph Murphy

MEDITATION THERAPY

Think a new thought (repent), live in Me now (belief), see no lack, and there will be no illusion. Be My book fulfilling your own chapters.

Be noiseless. Listen to your voice, which is My whisper. Learn of Me. Feel My being until you lose all that you thought was you, realizing it is really I.

Hush, seek and obey My voice. Release your selfdom as we do this together and watch Me give you the keys to My kingdom, which was lost within. All of the universe is waiting for your unlocking.

ꙮ Chapter 4 ꙮ

Broke

(Broke Song Artist Lecrae)

*"Beloved, do not believe every spirit, but test the spirits,
whether they are of God, because many false prophets have
gone out into the world."*

1 John 4:1 (NKJV)

RELIGIOUS SHACKLES CHALLENGE: YOUR FIVE SENSES

In Jesus' era, religion fought with his divinity because they refused to believe anything beyond their limited scope. They were walking by their five senses and living in their flesh through self-worship, pride, and relying on man's approval against God. They were emulating their father, – Lucifer. Jesus was both flesh (Jesus) and spirit (Christ). Unlike all other humans, he came through no man's fleshy seed but through a spiritual seed – the Holy Spirit *(Matthew 1:18)*.

As the story goes, Mary was a virgin and engaged to Joseph when she had a visitation from the angels of the Lord. The angels told her the Holy Spirit would come upon her, and God's spirit will overtake her and make her pregnant with a child. This is the mystery of God's supernatural wonders. Do not try to figure this out with your natural senses but rather with the invisible senses called faith.

Lucifer had lost his spiritual power; thus, he hated the spiritual self of Jesus. This rebellious spirit lives on today as the shackles of religion play tricks on your mind through the physical five senses so you can become spiritually blinded to God's discernment and spiritually deaf to what he is saying to you from within. God wants you to use your spiritual senses and know His voice, so you will not be led to the slaughterhouse making everything and everyone on the outside your God. Still, when failure comes, you blame God. But it was your lack of knowledge of who you are in God and who God is in you that is to blame.

You choose to continue refusing His voice that knocks at your heart to enter. You chose this even when your spiritual leader touched you inappropriately, knowing that it felt wrong. You chose this while willingly entering an affair. You are letting your selfish desires override God's voice and the voice of the prophets He sends your way to warn you. Then you say to yourself, "I thought that was God." "Why me, God?" How could you have known when you never stopped and looked for God within yourself?

> *"My sheep hear My voice, and I know them, and they follow Me."*
>
> *John 10:27 (NKJV)*

SPIRITUAL SOVEREIGNTY SOLUTION: YOUR INVISIBLE SENSES

> *"God is a Spirit: and they that worship him must worship him in spirit and in truth."*
>
> *John 4:24 (KJV)*

One In A Million You

Know that you are more than just a physical body. You are a spirit, and to worship God, you must do so by the spirit because God is Spirit. Yes, your physical body can do the act of worship, but real worship is from *you-spirit* to *God-Spirit,* and this is the truth. How do you do this type of worship? From within. Your spiritual helmet of salvation is your armor against the enemy's spiritual warfare. It protects your invisible mind from the illusions trying to reach it by way of your five senses. Once your helmet filters out the bad news, the word of God will come to slice, dice, and pierce the lies. He will replace the lies with the truth in your invisible mind. Your mind is your playscript – given to you by God to produce, direct, and cast the characters in your play according to your desires.

Whose script are you staring at? God's or your enemy? Spiritually sovereign souls study their Father God's manuscript (Bible), not only to learn about their maker but to learn how to manifest your promised land through what God has already created for you. You choose how your manuscript plays from your invisible senses within. You choose the enemy. You choose the lead. And, you can change the script. Learn to write the script. The graveyard is filled with countless names of those who did not know how to play their role in the game of life.

"Stand fast therefore in the liberty wherewith Christ hath made us free, and be not entangled again with the yoke of bondage."

Galatians 5:1 (KJV)

Spiritual Sovereignty Action

Produce your own promise land by rewriting your old life's play script!

SELF-WHISPER EXERCISE

1. Do you know God's voice?

2. Do you believe that God comes from within you and why?

3. Who has been writing your life play?

4. What role have you been allowing yourself to play up 'til now?

MEDITATION QUOTES

"Sovereignty is living from your spiritual senses; Religion is living from your five senses."

Phyllis Y Whitley

"I grew up like a neglected weed – ignorant of liberty, having no experience of it."

Harriet Tubman

"Nothing comes from without, all things come from within."

Neville Goddard

MEDITATION THERAPY

I Am your Teacher and Counselor, your Tutor and Advisor, your Redeemer and Rescuer, your Protector and Healer, your Guide and Driver, your Mother and Father, your Sister and Brother, your Friend and Business Partner, your Doctor and Lawyer, your Architect and Accountant. I Am waiting for you to accept and believe in Me to express and show Myself exceedingly through you from within.

Complete the sentence and become who you see yourself becoming:

I am...(your career)

I am...(your income)

I am...(your emotion)

I am...(your relationship)

I am...(your personality)

I am...(your hobby)

❦ Chapter 5 ❦

Gangster Paradise

(Gangster Paradise Song Artist 2 Pac)

"For false Christ and false prophets will rise and show great signs and wonders to deceive, if possible, even the elect."

Matthew 24:24 (NKJV)

RELIGIOUS SHACKLES CHALLENGE: WOLVES LIVING QUARTERS

Countless spiritual wolf headquarters are setting up shop in the spiritual realm waiting to embody anything or anyone in low to high places for opposing God's truth and stealing His praise. For centuries, these hypocrites have been planting seeds. They have been shacking up and taken living quarters in our churches and spiritual communities as lovers of lies, rape, molestation, and various other sexually immoral acts performed by your very own spiritual leaders and other leaders of different industries. Unfortunately, these radical religious shackles listed below prey on the young, the innocent, and the ignorant early in life to destroy their faith in God, causing many to give up on their dream early as they answer to the invitation of the grave.

- **Churches** – an entity of spiritual leaders called to slaughter their shepherds and keep out God's true anointed children while the religious shackles seeds continue to multiply, devouring innocent members from generation to generation, keeping them further from God.

- **Political** – a large stage to implement and create ungodly laws where greedy power and selfish desires are played on the capitol hill reality show.
- **Education** – a system to keep prayer out of school (God's covering) and not allowing the children to recognize that they are more than just a physical being but also a spirit.
- **Music** – a popular industry with lyrics that does nothing to build your spirit but to place too much emphasis upon our lacks.
- **Media** – a negative platform of commercial advertisement, books, magazines, and movies catered to lowering your morality, culture, and your true identity.
- **Social Media** – the negative everything that feeds your five senses illusions.
- **Food Industry** – catering to gluttony, food, and drinks that destroy your temple.
- **Medical Community** – producer of a pharmaceutical community creating a mass of harmful drugs while causing greedy doctors to become the largest drug pusher of prescriptive medicine, feeding the symptoms that heal no one but causes long-term codependent behavior avoiding the root cause of the illness.
- **Home** – a place of secrecy, where abuse, incest, and rape among the family occur in your years of innocence, before recognizing you are a spirit, not just flesh, that could destroy your life's purpose.
- **Streets** – are the drug pushers, pimps, preachers, rapists, molesters, or racist people. Spirits that stunt your growth, stop your dreams and lead you to a limited space called jail.

SPIRITUAL SOVEREIGNTY SOLUTION: MASTER GOD'S MANUSCRIPT

"Who shall separate us from the love of Christ? Shall tribulation, or distress, or persecution, or famine, or nakedness, or peril, or sword?"

Romans 8:35 (KJV)

You Are Everything, and Everything is You!

You might have felt like you have been through hell and back due to being abused one time or another in your life by someone you trusted. This can leave a scar on you mentally and physically. Even more devastating is the abuse by a spiritual leader you believed was the next best person to God. Undoubtedly, you paid the price, and now you are scared spiritually. You are left in a place of shame, embarrassment, and even hatred towards God and yourself – right where those religious shackles wanted you to be.

First, you must immediately know that you are not alone in this matter because many of us were deceived or disappointed by a spiritual leader at some point in life. Therefore, God said his children would perish or be destroyed due to a lack of knowledge. He wants you to know who He really is, but you must learn His manuscript for yourself.

God's manuscript will give you an up-close look at the false leaders and how to discern their nature based on their heart and spirit and not their foolish teachings and sayings that will come back to choke them. This is where you see countless leaders fall every day. Spiritual sovereignty soaks you in God's word to a point you become Him, and He becomes you. This is true oneness. He is waiting for you to accept Him wholeheartedly until He can express Himself fully through you. His Loving Spirit of discernment will operate through you as a human vessel to reveal the real spiritual gangsters hiding in your church.

Listen to God's still voice as He moves you forward to your special promise land where He can direct your path from bondage to freedom, from hurt to healing, from humiliated to honor, and from faithless to faithful.

Teach your children early on about God and fill yourself with the knowledge of His word. You will see that no darkness could ever separate you from God. He is that wonderful shadow that has always been a part of you. It becomes magnified in daylight because God is light. Have you ever wondered why your shadow is bigger than you? Now you know.

God knows everything and sees everything because He is everything. Why would you continue to worship and believe in illusions when right inside you is a God that will never steal your joy or innocence or violate your dignity. It is time to release those religious chains of darkness and take back your power by building up your greatness through spiritual sovereignty practices, so your life's script will not be found on the wayside destroyed.

> *"Ye are of God, little children, and have overcome them: because greater is he that is in you, than he that is in the world."*
>
> *1 John 4:4 (KJV)*

Spiritual Sovereignty Action

Direct your new life's play by mastering God's manuscript!

SELF-WHISPER EXERCISE

1. What industry has played a significant part in your view of God?

2. Whose life play have you put your trust in and why?

3. What actions can you take to look past the hurt?

MEDITATION QUOTES

"If you want to know about everything and everybody become skilled with God's manuscript."

Phyllis Y. Whitley

"Discipline has within its potential for creating future miracles."

Jim Rohn

MEDITATION THERAPY

I release all religious shackles in my life's play.
I now let God produce my life's play.
I forgive those who willfully misguided my spiritual walk as I fire each character.
I forgive myself for believing in outside gods.
I replace my old religious shackles with divine spiritual sovereignty.
I am a unique spiritual being having an extraordinary human life role.
I rewrite my script by choosing my rightful role and the right characters.
Thank you, my innermost God!

☙ Chapter 6 ☙

Church Clothes

(Church Clothes Song Artist Lecrae)

"Beware of false prophets, which come to you in sheep's clothing, but inwardly they are ravening wolves."

Matthew 7:15 (KJV)

RELIGIOUS SHACKLES CHALLENGE: CHURCH HURT

You thought it was the members in your church that hurt you, no! It was an inside job. Those hidden (invisible) religious spirits were bringing you seeds showing up as shackles, iron, chains, bonds, restraint, and handcuffs to keep you from doing the divine work of God within you. Let me make it plain. The heavy restrictions and limitations in your mind, body, and soul are religious spirits operating around you to keep your eyes on a remote God, demanding your religious worship instead of sacred spiritual growth. Their actions can recognize today's hypocritical spirits:

Belief in an outside God.	Belief that hard struggle pleases God.
Judges everyone from the outside.	Fearful of the spiritual world.
Talk religious but live unrighteously.	Seek men's approval, not God.

Preach fear base Bible stories	Allergic to miracles and prophets.
Focus on strict religious traditions.	Walk by sight, not by faith.
Unbelief in Jesus Christ as Lord.	Seek outward signs and wonders.
Give all praises to themselves only.	Belief they are the only righteous church
Critical toward God real anointed people.	Belief that Godly poverty is a virtue
Prey on the vulnerable & elderly	Do not practice what they preach

Today, these religious shackles seem to love the institution of the church. Yes! I said it! Because these spirits lead church members to believe that holiness means having a spiritual title, wearing a holy outfit, or trying to be seen carrying their unread Bible. In truth, their outward appearances are all they have since their insides are void of God's presence. Unfortunately, the only way you can tell is by the spirit of discernment, which allows you to look at their hearts and know them by their rotten fruits labeled as a rapist, molester, cheater, and greedy.

Religious shackles love to live a life of overfeeding their flesh, not understanding that they are in darkness and unable to see the light. That is why they will do everything to hide your light as they tried with Jesus. In due season their wickedness will be exposed. The next time you find yourself chasing and worshiping another because they look holy, look again. They might be wolves in sheep's clothing. You might want to remember this when choosing your next spiritual leader or life mate.

*"You will know them by their fruits. Do men gather grapes
from thornbushes or figs from thistles?"*

Matthew 7:16 (NKJV)

SPIRITUAL SOVEREIGNTY SOLUTION: SOUL FOOD

*But the fruit of the Spirit is love, joy, peace, longsuffering,
kindness, goodness, faithfulness, gentleness, self-control.
Against such there is no law.*

Galatians 5:22-23

Body and Soul

God's intention is for you to live a kingdom life by being attentive
to your spiritual being, not just your physical being alone. It is crucial
to know the importance of choosing to feed yourself spiritual food
through *prayer, fasting, meditation, reading the word, daydreaming,*
and *affirmations*. Feeding your spiritual being is just like feeding your
physical being. Just as your physical being needs a variety of
nourishing food for growth and development, so too does your
spiritual being. Depending on what is being fed to your spirit, the
process will yield or manifest a good crop or a bad one. A true
spiritual leader will feed you good news (gospel), knowing that your
fruit shall speak for itself in time.

A Spiritual Sovereign person loves feeding on soul food as he or
she learns to master their spiritual wellbeing. Therefore, their spiritual
being will never go hungry for nutrition; else, your physical flesh will
have a field day overpowering your spirit through its corrupt, selfish
cravings. For optimal enhancement, use God's manuscript as your
daily feeding to your spiritual being. This act will visibly manifest on
your stage play called life. However, if you continue feeding your

flesh, you will attract the big bad wolf, and he will take over your life play and call it religion.

> *"For the flesh lusts against the Spirit, and the Spirit against the flesh; and these are contrary to one another, so that you do not do the things that you wish."*

> *Galatians 5:17 (NKJV)*

Spiritual Sovereignty Action

Feed your spirit soul food!

SELF-WHISPER EXERCISE

1. What hypocritical spirits have you been harboring?

2. Are the leaders in your life showing evidence of a sovereign being or a hypocrite?

3. What can you do to grow and develop your spiritual being?

MEDITATION QUOTES

> *"Feed your spirit soul food and your flesh living food."*

> *Phyllis Y. Whitley*

"Our only limitations are those we set up in our own minds."

Napoleon Hill

MEDITATION THERAPY

I now bring myself to higher consciousness.
I manifest unlimited benefits in my health.
I manifest unlimited benefits in my career.
I manifest unlimited benefits in my relationships.
I manifest unlimited benefits in my education.
I can see it, I can feel it, I can hear it developing within my spiritual darkroom of imagination now.
Gratitude and thanks to my unlimited God within.

❧ Chapter 7 ❧

Not Today Satan!

(Not Today Satan Song Artist KB)

"and said, "O full of all deceit and all fraud, you son of the devil, you enemy of all righteousness, will you not cease perverting the straight ways of the Lord?"

Acts 13:10 (NKJV)

RELIGIOUS SHACKLES CHALLENGE: THE THREE D'S

Religious shackles come in the same form as what many religious Christians call the devil. However, Christians give too much credit to the devil's name, meditating day and night on all the wrong he has caused. The next time you keep meditating on the phrase "devil," you will attract the devil manifested as the three D's (Doubt, Division, Debt).

1. **Doubt** – will have you second-guessing God. *"But let him ask in faith, with no doubting, for he who doubts is like a wave of the sea driven and tossed by the wind.*[7] *For let not that man suppose that he will receive anything from the Lord;*[8] *he is a double-minded man, unstable in all his ways." (James 1:6-8, NKJV)*
2. **Division** – will have you thinking that God is separated from you when He is within you. *"Who shall separate us from the love of Christ? Shall tribulation, or distress, or persecution,*

or famine, or nakedness, or peril, or sword?" (Romans 8:35, NKJV)

3. **Debt** – will keep you as a slave serving money. *"No one can serve two masters; for either he will hate the one and love the other, or else he will be loyal to the one and despise the other. You cannot serve God and mammon." (Matthew 6:24, NKJV)*

The other name that is whispered day and night is "enemy." Remember when you were experiencing a storm in your life, and someone asked you how you were doing? Your neck turned like the lady in the exorcist, and immediately you answered, "the enemy is busy." You did hear the word enemy; well, that really means "inner me." Take a moment and think about it. Then ask yourself if you had ever seen that so-called red devil with horns besides the one on your hot sauce bottle? No. Yet you meditate on that name morning, noon, and night and wonder why you are reaping hell.

The religious shackles are bondage spirits disguised as devilish thoughts, words, and emotions that keep you living your three D's – doubt, division, and debt. In the same way, once they move into your mind, they will try to take up permanent residency keeping your thoughts on regret, resentment, and revenge so your life's play can get canceled and all you have are reruns or a play that never made it past the pre-planning stage.

"Therefore, submit to God. Resist the devil and he will flee from you."

James 4:7 (NKJV)

SPIRITUAL SOVEREIGNTY SOLUTION: TRUE PROPHET

"For as he thinks in his heart, so is he."

Proverbs 23:7 (NKJV)

Heard It Through the Grapevine

Knowing who you really are is the beginning of becoming a spiritually sovereign soul. God does not just want you to read His manuscript as if it's another story. He wants you to see Him from a prophetic view, or should I say through the eyes of a prophet. The Bible is a book of God's relationships with His chosen prophets and how He shared His most heartfelt secrets with each one of them differently and yet the same. God's wondrous work was done through prophets in the Old Testament. Later in the New Testament, God led by example through the greatest prophet ever, Jesus Christ.

Many have said that prophets no longer exist today, but if you believe that God exists today, His prophets exist today. Prophets are God's mouthpiece, and since God is an Invisible Spirit, He needs a human body to use to do His work, greater, I must add. Is that not what Jesus said to his disciples after his resurrection? The bottom line is God already created everything, but He needs His prophets to manifest not only their own promised land but also that of everyone that needs salvation (saving from the illusion of lack).

How? Well, if you are a prophet, then you are God's mouthpiece, and what you speak must come to pass. So, what are you saying? Are your words saving or killing you? If you think gospel, then you will speak good news like a true prophet. But if you speak bad news (witchcraft, voodoo, curses, jinxes), then you are casting a spell upon yourself and others. That is a false prophet.

Possibly, could Lucifer have been a bad thought in God's mind?

Remember, God kicked Lucifer out of Heaven (mind), and now he is walking the earth to place his words in your mouth through your mind. Stop listening to the grapevine – a form of religious shackles. In the beginning, was the word, but where was the word before it started creating? It was in God's mind, and guess who was with Him? Lucifer saw it all, so he knows how powerful your word is because you are made in God's image, and God's word is also a seed. Therefore, your word will not return unto you void. Wow! This is one of the greatest secrets to manifesting your promised land. Are you a true prophet speaking God's words, or are you a false prophet speaking religion?

> *"Surely the Lord GOD does nothing, Unless He reveals His secret to His servants the prophets."*
>
> *Amos 3:7.(NKJV)*

Spiritual Sovereignty Action

Prophesy good news (gospel) to yourself!

SELF-WHISPER EXERCISE

1. What areas of your life have you manifested the three D's called doubt, division, and debt?

2. Are you paying attention to the thoughts you are allowing to play on repeat in your mind?

3. What spells are you prophesying to yourself?

MEDITATION QUOTES

"A mouth filled with cursing will manifest curses."

Phyllis Y. Whitley

"Our attitude towards life determines life's attitude towards us."

Earl Nightingale

MEDITATION THERAPY

I prophesy to myself:

— I let go of my past pain as I now walk in my true divine bliss.
— Every good dream of mine comes to fruition quickly.
— I now go within my imagination and see myself winning in the game of life.
— I am attracting the best specific people, places, and things into my experience.
— I desire wisdom and humbleness to handle my riches righteously.
— I rewrite my script every night to line up with happiness and peace.
— My inner self is jumping for joy every time I give birth to my amazing desires.
— I now unfold my unique God talents and gifts to become a blessing to all I meet.

Thank you, Divine Intelligent Father!

ꗞ Chapter 8 ꗞ

I'm Getting Ready

(I'm Getting Ready Song Artist Tasha Cobbs & Nicki Minaj)

"Woe to you, scribes and Pharisees, hypocrites! For you devour widows' houses, and for a pretense make long prayers. Therefore, you will receive greater condemnation."

Matthew 23:14 (NKJV)

RELIGIOUS SHACKLES CHALLENGE: PUBLIC PRAYER

Religious shackles will have you praying on every church altar and asking everybody outside of yourself to help you find God, hoping you gain worldly recognition so you can lose all hope in God and make man your god. You are living a life of ignorance. This is why so many religious leaders and their members reach a point of no return with unanswered prayers, inability to hear God's voice, and lack of faith as they walk away from a God they never really knew or had a relationship with.

God's power can only be found in that secret place – within. Since Jesus was at the beginning of God's creation, he understood that the secret place could be experienced through an intimacy called prayer early in the morning. He sought his Father first because he knew his divinity needed the right spiritual food.

Do you find yourself wondering why your prayers are not

answered? Could it be that you are praying to a god that does not exist at your church's altar? Or perhaps to a statue or painting that was created by the hands of man? Sunday after Sunday, you rush to your church prayer lines begging God over and over for the same thing. Consider your children. What if you brought food home from the supermarket only for your children to keep telling you they are hungry when there is plenty of food in the refrigerator? You might call the mental ward. This is how God feels. Listen! He has heard your prayers the first time.

Do not get me twisted. I am not saying going to a church altar for prayer is a bad thing. It is just not the only correct way to get God's attention. If it were, you would not be reading this book. Leaders today are afraid to preach or teach about anything too spiritual, so instead, they focus on your sins. When you continue to hear how sinful and dirty you are, you cannot help but cry out and run to the altar, asking God for forgiveness.

Praying in shame will only continue feeding your physical being, causing you to live a life of manifesting your pastor's or teacher's message of sin because you eventually become what you think about. As a result, your leader might wonder why sin is all in his house. Because he practiced what he preached and taught all his members to believe they are nothing but sinners going to hell. You both will reap what you believe in *until* you learn what real prayer is.

> *"Therefore, I say to you, whatever things you ask when you pray, believe that you receive them, and you will have them."*
>
> *Mark 11:24 (NKJV)*

SPIRITUAL SOVEREIGNTY SOLUTION: INTIMACY WITHIN

*"But you, beloved, building yourselves up on your most holy
faith, praying in the Holy Spirit keep yourselves in the love of
God, looking for the mercy of our Lord Jesus Christ unto
eternal life."*

Jude 1:20-21 (NKJV)

The Closer I Get to You

First, God said you must believe it is yours when you pray, and
you will have it. Further on, believing is living like you have what
you are asking God for NOW. Play the real role you want to be as if
you presently have it. Prayer is one of your spiritual foods that will
build your spiritual self to the highest realization level when it is done
within your invisible self.

In the same way, God wants you to go into your mind and shut
your five senses (your outside world) and have an intimate
conversation about your dream desires with Him, within your
invisible mind (unseen from others). God will then manifest your
sacred desires on the outside of yourself where others can finally see
it.

Now, do you understand why most of your prayers went
unanswered? Try having a real relationship with God and watch what
happens when your spirit weaves with God's Spirit and become one.
You will give birth to your promised land right in front of your
religious friends and family members. Yet, out of their ignorance,
they will say, "That's not God!"

"But thou, when thou prayest, enter into thy closet, and when thou hast shut thy door, pray to thy Father which is in secret; and thy Father which seeth in secret shall reward thee openly."

Matthew 6:6

Spiritual Sovereignty Action

Pray to God in secrecy (within).

SELF-WHISPER EXERCISE

1. Have you been relying on others to pray for you?

2. Have you been praying to God secretly within or publicly at your church altar?

3. Are you praying with gratitude or conviction?

4. Are you believing that God has answered your prayers? Are you acting out your script as though you are your desires now?

MEDITATION QUOTES

"Praying in your heavenly language is likens unto an instant message to God."

Phyllis Y. Whitley

"God is the presence and power within you, right now. God is the mastermind working through you now."

Dr. Frederick Eikerenkoetter

MEDITATION THERAPY

I am…

P – prosperous in all things
R – royal priesthood
A – advancing towards my higher self
Y – Yahweh within
E – extraordinarily humbled
R – revising my life play daily

ꙮ Chapter 9 ꙮ

Not My Baby

(Not My Baby Song Artist Bone Thugs-n-Harmony)

"So God created mankind in his own image, in the image of God he created them; male and female he created them."

Genesis 1:27 (NIV)

RELIGIOUS SHACKLES CHALLENGE: FALSE FATHER

You Look Like Your Father

Since God made man in His image, we cannot help but look like God. For example, when a baby is born, the first words out of a mother or father's mouth is "you look just like your...." Everyone is excited to see who the baby resembles. Likewise, the same goes for our Spiritual Father. Since God is a Spirit, our spirit should resemble Him.

If a baby does not look like the mother, it's not a big deal, but what happens if the baby doesn't look like daddy? You know what the old folks use to say, "mommy baby, daddy maybe." Perhaps, the mother is confused about who her real baby daddy is because she had several seeds deposited in her garden in the same month. If she is single, she might put it on the one who can support her; even more disputable, if married, she has no choice but to put it on her husband, taking her shame hush-hush to her grave.

God knows a woman's religious shackles choice will manifest a life of misery, shame, and heartbreak. He intended a woman to have one husband and protect her garden until she learns how to manifest her desired king. In fact, what happens to a flowerpot when you sow several different seeds in it? You will produce an undesirable mixture of flowers. Likewise, what happens to your spiritual being when you allow several different men to deposit a bundle of seeds into your garden? You just tied each of those men's spirits unto your spirit. It's called a soul-tie. In other words, every man you let into your garden is another soul connection that is hard to break. Now you know why you keep thinking and dreaming about your old rusty boyfriend, you broke up with decades ago, especially when an old song triggers your thoughts. It's because you are tangled until sovereignty purges your spirit.

Decade after decade, women sits alone on the sideline watching so-called worldly women meeting their husband in the marketplace. Religious shackled leaders will put your life in a box of doom waiting for your husband at your specific church and denomination when in fact, they are just hoping you bring another member to increase their low numbers and wallet. What happened? You made an agreement with your religious leader and then put your religion helmet on, waiting for the day God will bring your husband to the church.

Despite what you have been told, your church is not the only place to meet your husband. If it was, then why are there so many divorces occurring in the church community? Sadly, countless religious women who gave their power to their shackled leader wind up with an uncontrollable flesh, left their church, grew old and missed their childbearing years, died in idleness, or continued to become one flesh with their community of men.

"Therefore a man shall leave his father and mother and be joined to his wife, and they shall become one flesh."

Genesis 2:24 (NKJV)

SPIRITUAL SOVEREIGNTY SOLUTION: GARDEN PRUNING

"It is good for a man not to touch a woman. Nevertheless, because of sexual immorality, let each man have his own wife, and let each woman have her own husband. Let the husband render to his wife the affection due her, and likewise also the wife to her husband."

1 Corinthians 7:1-3 (NKJV)

My Secret Garden

Celibacy is a gift from God. Not everyone can live that life. I believe that a spiritual leader called by God should practice celibacy until they meet their life mate. This does not give a spiritual leader the license to become a shepherd slaughter slut or whoremongers. However, know that God is a forgiving God that wants you to be happy if you wish to marry or not.

Be wise and do not allow everyone to touch your secret garden nor have easy access to it, for this will lead to all types of fleshly desires that will manifest into fleshly corruption. God wants to be your spiritual spouse so that He can spoil you. He wants to show you how you should be treated and how you should treat your physical spouse and not sell yourself short when your real spouse shows up.

"He who finds a wife finds a good thing, and obtains favor from the Lord."

Proverbs 18:22 (NKJV)

Activate your spiritual sovereignty and come out of the soul ties cycle by putting a mental sign on your garden that says, "spouse only." Meanwhile, keep busy playing your ultimate life role, and you will attract like-minded people to your stage play. God has given you the power to choose the characters you want, so ladies, be choosy like a virtuous woman and lead by example for other women you allow into your life. Whether you want a spouse or not, a spiritually sovereign woman cultivates both her physical and spiritual garden in seven ways:

Physical	Spiritual
Planting – choosing which seeds are allowed into your garden	Planting – choosing which seeds are allowed into your five senses (gate)
Watering – washing gently with a natural product daily.	Watering – washing gently with gospel affirmations
Fertilizing– eating healthy (live) food for good nutrition from the inside out.	Fertilizing– eating healthy (live) soul food by meditating on the gospel (good news) you want to happen.
Sunlight – implement a good vitamin D into your healthy regimen along with some natural sunlight.	Sunlight – master God's word so it can shine through you.

Air – exercise while using good breathing techniques.	Air– exercise your imagination through mental pictures of your promised land.
Temperature – keeping a healthy pH balanced body	Temperature – keeping a healthy pH balanced mind.
Pruning – implementing a good pre/probiotic supplement and preventive care checkups for weeding out toxins in the body.	Pruning–implementing a good coach or counselor to assist you in weeding away your past pain and reshaping your future.

"He shall be like a tree planted by the rivers of water, that brings forth its fruit in its season, whose leaf also shall not wither; and whatever he does shall prosper."

Psalms 1:3 (NKJV)

Sovereign Solution

Cultivate your garden for your husband

SELF-WHISPER EXERCISE

1. Do you truly know who your Father is?

2. Have you wisely allowed the right seeds to be sown into your life?

3. Would you choose yourself as a role model based on your life's

choices?

4. How will you incorporate all seven steps to cultivate your garden?

MEDITATION QUOTES

"Respecting your garden ladies means not allowing every penis to sow into it."

"Too many seeds in a woman's garden produces a weed of soul ties."

Phyllis Y. Whitley

MEDITATION THERAPY

I am now taking charge of my ultimate self.
I am enriching my garden every day by keeping a watch on my garden gate.
I am using my God-given power to choose the right characters for my fruitful life play.
I have decided to end soul-tie cycles and embrace my first love, God.
God is teaching me what a real king is because He is the King of kings.
While I am busy producing my play, I am attracting my soulmate, who is really me.

Thank you, Father!

☙ Chapter 10 ☙

Scandalous

(Scandalous Song Artist Prince)

"Ye are of your father the devil, and the lusts of your father ye will do. He was a murderer from the beginning, and abode not in the truth, because there is no truth in him. When he speaketh a lie, he speaketh of his own: for he is a liar, and the father of it."

John 8:44.(KJV)

RELIGIOUS SHACKLES CHALLENGE: CHURCH MOLESTERS

Religious shackles love to disguise themselves as religious leaders in the church community titled Bishop, Apostle, Pastor, Evangelist, and Prophet; even as servants under these leaders such as deacons, elders, lead worshipers, secretaries, and department leaders. Their tasks are to fool everyone with their titles and to keep God's anointed children out of the church building so they can play church as religious rapists, phony prophets, or pulpit pimps devouring the congregation. Religious shackles have turned the new churches into a business reality show called "**Manipulated Money Market Molesters**."

A friend once mentioned to me about God's calling. She said, "Few are chosen, but many went anyway." I later found out how true this is as the world watches our trusted religious leaders being carried away to prison more often than a bank robber. They are making headlines more often than actors. You may ask yourself, "What is going on?" Realize that these religious shackles have been out since their father Lucifer fell from Heaven with his angels. They have been lying and deceiving the masses' minds, causing many church members to seek the spiritual underground for answers from *witches, priestesses, sorcerers, psychics, and voodoo doctors* because no one ever told them about God's power within.

> *"Also he caused his sons to pass through the fire in the Valley of the Son of Hinnom; he practiced soothsaying, used witchcraft and sorcery, and consulted mediums and spiritists. He did much evil in the sight of the Lord, to provoke Him to anger."*
>
> 2 Chronicles 33:6 (NKJV)

SPIRITUAL SOVEREIGNTY SOLUTION: NEW DNA

> *"The mind governed by the flesh is death, but the mind governed by the Spirit is life and peace."*
>
> Roman 8:6 (NIV)

Love Under New Management

Religious shackle leaders are being devoured because they allow their flesh to regulate their minds. Still, the spiritual sovereign lives in their promised land of milk and honey because they know how to regulate their mind. Be wary of chasing the underworld of illusions for the answers. All your answers are in you. You have a mediator named Jesus Christ who came to show you what divinity looks like in you. It is you and God agreeing through your mind and speech that bring you into oneness with Him. Think Christ-mind and live like you want to be by thinking you are already what you desire to be. Become legitimate by putting on your helmet of salvation, which will save you from a limited mind so you can begin to walk in your new spiritual DNA called Divine-New Covenant of Abundance.

> *"And for this reason, He is the Mediator of the new covenant, by means of death, for the redemption of the transgressions under the first covenant, that those who are called may receive the promise of eternal inheritance."*
>
> *Hebrews 9:15 (NKJV)*

Spiritual Sovereignty Action

Live in your new spiritual DNA through your abundant mind now!

SELF-WHISPER EXERCISE

1. From whom are you seeking your answers?

2. Can you see that the answers you are seeking come from God within?

3. Are you allowing God to speak to you or other gods?

MEDITATION QUOTES

"True Christianity is having a Christ consciousness that leads by example."

Phyllis Y. Whitley

"A man is literally what he thinks, his character being the complete sum of all his thoughts."

James Allen

MEDITATION THERAPY

— I decree and declare that I am a happy, healthy, wise, fun-loving, patient, humble, and prosperous being.
— I decree and declare that I am a loving light unto all I encounter virtually, physically, and spiritually.
— I decree and declare I am attracting like-minded beings as we all love, live, and laugh in God's oneness.
— I decree and declare that my mind is full of abundance saving me from the illusion of lack.
— I decree and declare that I am love, living under new management.

Thank you, Divine Glory within me!

☙ Chapter 11 ☙

Daddy's Home

(Daddy's Home Song Artist Jackson 5)

*"Now when Jehu had come to Jezreel, Jezebel heard of it;
and she put paint on her eyes and adorned her head and
looked through a window."*

2 Kings 9:30 (NKJV)

RELIGIOUS SHACKLES CHALLENGE: JEZEBEL

Remember back in the days within the old holiness church when so-called holy women were not allowed to wear makeup and dress sexy otherwise, they would be looked down upon and called a Jezebel. Inappropriately, those old and some current churches took this scripture out of perspective because painting her face was not the reason why Jezebel displeased God. She was a prophetess assassinator, and she dabbled in witchcraft. Yes, she hated God's word so, she went after his precious mouthpiece called the prophet. It is no wonder Jezebel reaped a terrible death by the word of prophet Elijah *"On the plot of ground at Jezreel dogs shall eat the flesh of Jezebel"* (2 King 9:36, NKJV)

Jezebel is another vicious spirit disguised as religious shackles that are still fooling many women today, leaving them thinking that Father God will only bless the holy dressed and frequent churchgoers with a husband. Is this why spiritual men usually choose wives outside the church leaving countless women with baffled feelings and frustrated with God that their prayers were never answered? Ask yourself, ladies, did God tell you to claim every man who visits your church? Did God tell you to pray and wait for your married pastor to leave his wife? Did God tell you to shack up with every male and female because you had no flesh-control and felt lonely? No! That vicious voice you heard through your pastor or in your head was a seed of Jezebel's spirit, killing your prophetic voice and sight.

This Jezebel spirit wants to steal your spiritual sight, focusing on your loneliness and killing your voice. Soon, your speech is consumed with that of a spouse due to the lack of one. Therefore, you stay idle decade after decade, waiting to be rescued by a soulmate. Meanwhile, the real virtuous women are in the marketplace excelling in their higher self because she can see and speak into her future, bringing it to her now, manifesting her life's play.

"Charm is deceitful and beauty is passing, But a woman who fears the LORD, she shall be praised.

Proverbs 31:30 (NKJV)

SPIRITUAL SOVEREIGNTY SOLUTION: BEAUTY TREATMENTS

"During the year before each young woman's turn to go to King Ahasuerus, the harem regulation required her to receive beauty treatments with oil of myrrh for six months and then with perfumes and cosmetics for another six months."

Esther 2:12 (CSB)

Heaven Must Be Missing An Angel

A virtuous woman is not a woman who goes to church but a woman who has the church within her that is God. How you treat God determines the type of man you will attract since God should be your first husband. As you learn all about God, you will master man because he was made in God's image. They are like-minded. As you get in the habit of putting God first through prayer, praise, and private time He will give you beauty treatments just as Esther was given for six months before she met her king.

Despite what your shackled leader told you, most men are visual, so there is nothing wrong with looking beautiful on the outside. However, do not put all your net worth on your head and body. Yes, ladies, if you must wear hair extensions to enhance your beauty, do so without using the whole bag of horsehair on your head. Trust me!

Finally, mothers should teach their young daughters how to live a spiritually sovereign life that will teach them to be ready for leadership, ownership, and wife consciousness so she can bring more than her beautiful looks to a table within marriage and business. You attract who you are, not what you want. Use your prophetic voice (affirmations) to speak your heart's desire and match it with your prophetic sight (imagery) to see what you want on your inner dress. Knowing *your outer dress will attract him, but your inner dress will keep him.*

"Who can find a virtuous woman? for her price is far above rubies."

Proverbs 31:10 (KJV)

Spiritual Sovereignty Action

Purge yourself daily into becoming a virtuous woman

SELF-WHISPER EXERCISE

1. Is the Jezebel spirit lurking in your church? How?

2. Are you working on beautifying your inner spirit? How?

3. What have you done for God to show Him that you are prepared for your king? Queen?

4. What have you done to advance your physical and spiritual status?

MEDITATION QUOTES

"If loving Self is right, you don't want to be wrong."

Phyllis Y. Whitley

"If I am not good to myself, how can I expect anyone else to be good to me?"

Maya Angelou

MEDITATION THERAPY

I release all the religious shackles in my life.

I now go to my Kingdom market within to buy all my spiritual makeup.

I now feed my mind with good soul food of thoughts.

I am now walking in my spiritual sovereignty abundance.

I am the person God ordained me to be.

I am using my mind to create my fabulous spouse and children.

My family will be my first platform to witness God's greatness.

I allow nothing but the best to enter the gates of my ears and eyes,

And I wear only the best spiritual apparel.

I am my own candle of light.

I walk it, I talk it, I see it

Who am I?

They all call me bless!

But you can call me virtuous.

Amen!

Proverbs 31:10:31

🍃 **Chapter 12** 🍃

I Got the Power!

(I Got the Power Song Artist Snap)

"For the kingdom of God is not in word, but in power."

1 Corinthians 4:20 (KJV)

RELIGIOUS SHACKLES CHALLENGE: UNAWARENESS

Nothing can be changed from the outside world. Therefore, take off your religious shackles and stop trying to change the world when all creation was made from the invisible realm (within) and is waiting for you to manifest it into the physical. Manifestation starts from your mind and what is felt with emotion goes through your spirit. That is why many non-religious people experience more success in manifestation. Some other religions embrace the power of meditation with affirmations and visualization better than most Christians because they were taught nothing about their own spirit except that their spirit might make it to Heaven.

Ironically, many religious Christians are afraid of their spiritual side or are ignorant of that side. Many are unaware of their own invisible being. Maybe this is why they call anything that looks like spirit the devil. For the same reason, the religious sectors questioned Jesus when he manifested everything from his inner powers. Watch out for that Jezebel spirit that wants to kill your sight and speech by keeping you in darkness, relying on your physical five senses, worshiping the shackled leaders because you thought they were the only one who had the power.

SPIRITUAL SOVEREIGNTY SOLUTION: AUTHORIZING

"And concerning the work of My hands, you command Me."

Isaiah 45:11 (NKJV)

Just My Imagination

The real secret is that you are God's authorized users, and you were given the promise and permission to manifest whatever your heart's desire by commanding (authorizing) God by way of your inner sight and speech (affirmation & visualization). Our endless Father gave us dominion over the works of our hands that can be readily accessed through spiritual sovereignty soul food. Stop looking for a God to come down on earth to re-create what was done already. Know that your spirit is His exact duplicate covered in a limited body. Yes! This is also why you must become the tools or products you desire to manifest it.

For example, a painter must become his or her brush as they began to paint the whole picture that was within, or a sports player must become his or her ball first. This is the beginning and end of controlling your imagery until you see your desire come to life and speak back to you on your life stage. Be patient. In due season your desires (good or bad) will manifest themselves. Know that what you picture in your mind now will show up in your future later, so think and speak the gospel (good news).

"For the vision is yet for an appointed time; But at the end it will speak, and it will not lie. Though it tarries wait for it; Because it will surely come, It will not tarry."

Habakkuk 2:3 (NKJV)

Spiritual Sovereignty Action

Command God through your power of imagination.

SELF-WHISPER EXERCISE

1. What are your feelings concerning meditation? How can you deal with those feelings?

2. What can you see yourself become?

3. Can you feel yourself become your manifestation?

MEDITATION QUOTES

"Idleness is a deadly screenshot; action is power."

Phyllis Y. Whitley

"By thought, the thing you want is brought to you; by action, you receive it."

Wallace D. Wattles

MEDITATION THERAPY

I am enjoying every minute of our luxury European cruise vacation with friends and family. Yesterday we explored the land of castles and kings; it was breathtaking.

I can see how immense and regal the old castles stood and the beautiful rooms kings once lived in.

We are having a wonderful time sightseeing. Oh, look at those beautiful statues!

I am feeling warmth, love, and happiness all at the same time.

I can hear everyone laughing with joy as we all walk back to our luxury suites.

I cannot keep my eyes off the beautiful ocean view from our large balcony. I can smell the ocean water and hear the peaceful waves.

Oh, hear someone knocking at our cabin door. It is room service delivering our family dinner.

It smells so good! I cannot wait to eat with my family. I am so full now and ready to end our night.

This has been one of my many fantastic vacations. I cannot also wait to tour Rome, Florence, and Venice tomorrow.

This whole trip filled me with so much joy and peace.

Thank you, innermost High God, for sharing your treasures with us!

☙ Chapter 13 ☙

Limitless

(Limitless Song Artist Jon Keith)

*"And the lord commended the unjust steward because he had
done wisely: for the children of this world are in their
generation wiser than the children of light."*

Luke 16:8 (KJV)

RELIGIOUS SHACKLES CHALLENGE: WORLDLY WISDOM

While many of the religious shackles were robbing the souls of
church leaders in the pulpit, during the 1800 and 1900s, there were
new-thought writers and teachers such as Florence Scovel Shinn,
Neville Goddard, Joseph Murphy, Napoleon Hill, and James Allen
who helped millions of people change their mindset through the word
of God. Likewise, current and past motivational speakers include
names like Les Brown, Brian Tracy, Jim Rohn, Wayne Dyer, who did
not hold positions in the pulpit and used their voices to change
countless people for the better.

Once upon a time, the old church ridiculed anyone teaching
without a church platform or those who did not have a bible in their
hands? Looking at today, many spiritual leaders sound more and more
like the old mystics and motivational speakers more than ever before.
Could it be that the children of the light are going through the
backdoor to learn success from the children of the world while their

church members remain in conscious poverty?

SPIRITUAL SOVEREIGNTY SOLUTION: MANIFEST

"Thou shalt also decree a thing, and it shall be established unto thee: and the light shall shine upon thy ways."

Job 22:28 (KJV)

If This World Were Mine

The new-thought age leaders taught people how to think again at a higher level by using their mental and spiritual activity. Similarly, motivational speakers excel at people's emotional and mental beings by inspiring them to embrace abundant life opportunities while overcoming adverse limitations. Even with much-proven success, religious shackles make you think that any man or woman not in the pulpit is of the devil when, in fact, it is the opposite. In truth, they were able to tap into a world of the abundant life that most religious shackle's leaders were afraid to touch – the unseen world. There is no need to sit inside a church building hearing about the laws of your flesh, *sinning*, every week until you find yourself in a revolving door manifesting sin after sin, living in a world of damnation.

Spiritual sovereignty beings motivate themselves through their spiritual, mental activity as they decree (seek) the good they desire. By going within their hearts (knock), using their five spiritual senses to see it, hear it, smell it, taste it, and touch it on the imaginary stage called your imagination, they learn how to manifest. Make sure you rehearse (meditate) your play lines daily until it is manifested as God shines (open) it back to you on your stage's play regardless if you have a platform or not.

"Ask, and it will be given to you; seek, and you will find; knock, and it will be opened to you."

Matthew 7:7 (NKJV)

Spiritual Sovereignty Action

Decree your good desires through your five spiritual senses.

SELF-WHISPER EXERCISE

1. Are your spiritual teachings helping you to live a successful life?

2. Do you see where you are living in a cycle of damnation?

3. Are you going within yourself and using your five senses to bring your desired new reality to the physical?

MEDITATION QUOTES

"Imagination is the house of your spiritual senses and your mind is the storage of your life blueprints."

Phyllis Y. Whitley

"An awakened imagination work with a purpose. It creates and conserves the desirable and transforms or destroys the undesirable."

Neville Goddard

MEDITATION THERAPY

I am liberated through truth and wisdom.
I am a magnet that attracts kingdom laws.
I am awakened to my true purpose.
I act as though I am that which my desire calls.
My words are cleansing my thoughts.
My thoughts are rinsing my mouth.
I am revealing the power within me.
My inward beauty is coming outward with a shout.
My respect toward others bounces back to me.
My tattoos are my unspoken words, so don't ask.
My scars are my testimonies with a key.
I am my unlimited supply reaching above the sky.
I am the greatness hidden within me.
I am my spirit supervisor that oversees.
Prayer is my fuel source every day.
My God is the producer of my play.
Relax! Because Mastermind Jesus has the final say.

☙ Chapter 14 ☙

I AM That I AM

(I Am That I Am Song Artist Cross Movement)

"And God said unto Moses, I AM THAT I AM: and he said, thus shalt thou say unto the children of Israel, I AM hath sent me unto you."

Exodus 3:14 (KJV)

RELIGIOUS SHACKLES CHALLENGE: GOD'S NAME

Let Your Real Name Change Your Address

Moses told the children of Israel God's actual name: *I Am That I Am*. Still, they continued to misuse His name because of their religious shackles mindset. How many of us were taught this truth in church or by our parents? Even when we first heard the word "I am," most of us probably did not know how much power is in that amazing name. The biggest misused name ever is God's name *I Am*.

Most religious leaders will reveal God's many names that they know of, but His "I Am" name was hidden from the carnal minded and only revealed through your spiritual sovereignty. What you say or think after His glorious name, "I Am," is your true nature. This is one of God's secrets to manifesting your tomorrow for good or bad. For example, *I am* successful, *I am* happy, *I am* tired, or *I am* lonely. What are you whispering to yourself? When you grab hold of this revelation, you will stop letting other people, circumstances, and feelings name your true nature.

SPIRIT SOVEREIGNTY SOLUTION: DIALOGUE ADJUSTMENT

"Let the weak say, 'I am strong.'"

Joel 3:10 (NKJV)

I Want to Know Your Name

Nevertheless, you will use God's name "I AM' daily because your I am-ness can't be separated from God's name, and whatever you put after His name will make you or break you, confirming that you and God are one. Think about how many times you said "I am" within a given day. Your inner or outer dialog will either speak life or death to you and uncover your current address (your position in life). Be wise in what you name yourself. This becomes your inner dialog of how you see yourself and how the world sees you too. Are you speaking low income or high income, job or your own business, rental or ownership, poverty, or prosperity?

Spiritual sovereignty is an immediate and daily changing of your outer and inner speech so you can change your spiritual address first, then your physical address will follow later. Understand this concept and know that God's name is in your everyday dialogue and that your words have the power to move you to your new address (promised land) or keep you in the wilderness like the Israelites.

Phyllis Y. Whitley

"Be still and know that I am God"

Psalm 46:10 (NKJV)

Spiritual Sovereignty Action

Name yourself who you want to be now to bring tomorrow into today.

SELF-WHISPER EXERCISE

1. What have you been calling yourself in the name of *I Am*? What was the effect you experienced?

2. Are you using the name "I Am" to identify your true nature? How?

3. What name have you whispered about other people on a daily basis?

MEDITATION QUOTES

"I am-ness is agreeing with God's words, excuses are fruitless words of nothingness."

Phyllis Y. Whitley

Be still! —and KNOW, —I AM, —GOD."

Joseph S. Benner

"Circumstances do not make a man, they reveal him."

Dr. Wayne Dyer

MEDITATION THERAPY

Thank you, El Shaddai, for being so almighty. You are my only El Elyon that cannot be copied because you are my master Adonai, yes Yahweh too. My actions are covered by my Jehovah Nissi, all wrapped up in one. Continue to shepherd me Jehovah Raah as you heal my old pain, Jehovah Rapha. I hear your righteousness Jehovah Tsidkenu and feel your sanctification Jehovah Mekoddishkem. My El Olam lives forever, and I am so glad you are my Elohim and my Qanna that let me know when you are jealous if I look outside of myself for you. No matter where I travel, I know that Jehovah Shammah is ahead of me because Jehovah Tsidkenu is purifying my steps. How astonished I am at my maker Elohim. Jehovah Jireh always provides for me while Jehovah Shalom shadow me with peace and blessings for my whole household. Thanks be to Jehovah Sabaoth!

Amen.

✌ Chapter 15 ✌

A House Is Not A Home

(A House is Not A Home Song Artist Luther Vandross)

"Even those men that did bring up the evil report upon the land, died by the plague before the LORD."

Numbers 14:37

RELIGIOUS SHACKLES CHALLENGE: WRONG ADDRESS

Regrettably, a forty-day trip to the promised land turned into a forty-year wilderness journey for the rebellious Israelites because of their religious shackles of faithlessness and complaining throughout their journey, even after witnessing God's many signs and wonders. The Israelites' final rebellious act occurred when a few were selected and sent by Moses to scout Canaan (the promised land). Many of the scouts saw a land filled with greatness but believed the people in that land were mightier than they were. The Israelites saw themselves as grasshoppers. Since they were afraid to take possession of the land, that whole community cried and wept that night and complained to Moses and Aaron within themselves. God noticed the negative report and was greatly displeased. Their bad report kept them at the wrong address, where some of them remained until death. Be careful what your whisper says about you; rather, it's loud or silent.

"The lips of the righteous feed many, But fools die for lack of wisdom."

Proverbs 10:21 (NKJV)

SPIRITUAL SOVEREIGNTY SOLUTION: CHANGE ADDRESS

"Finally, brethren, whatsoever things are true, whatsoever things are honest, whatsoever things are just, whatsoever things are pure, whatsoever things are lovely, whatsoever things are of good report; if there be any virtue, and if there be any praise, think on these things.

Philippians 4:8 (KJV)

Move Forward

It is time to change your address as Joshua and Caleb did. They scouted the land and returned with a good report of praise, truth, and pure thoughts pleasing to God. Their good news had yielded them both a great return – the promised land. Both Joshua and Caleb were just an example of not following the crowd but choosing to believe that God would give them the land. They were rewarded for their faithfulness and became the last two remnants of Egypt's Israelites allowed to enter a new address – a promised land.

Becoming spiritually sovereign means checking daily your inner and outer conversations with others and yourself, or it will return to you disguised as your giants of illness, debt, poverty, or fear. In short, let your new whisper move you to your new address, or should I say, "your promise land." *A man shall eat well by the fruit of his mouth, But the soul of the unfaithful feeds on violence (Proverbs 13:2, NKJV))*.

Spiritual Sovereignty Action

Change your mental address by thinking about the good report you desire.

SELF-WHISPER EXERCISE

1. At what address is your negative report keeping you?

2. Are you allowing others to take control of your good report?

3. Can you see where your past report determined your current address? How and why?

4. Can you see how people address reveals their inner whispers report?

5. Name two people that you admire that is living at a dream location?

6. Name two people who are living in an undesirable location. Are their whispers negative?

MEDITATION QUOTES

"Your physical address cannot be changed until you first change your whispers."

Phyllis Y. Whitley

"There is a supply for every demand."

Florence Scovel Shinn

MEDITATION THERAPY

I am that I am, visualizing my deep desire to come my way, but wait a minute, I heard that you were already here, so what do I do now? Wait or create? I think I will go within to find myself cleaning out the pollution and the clutter from my past tenants. Oh, how it hurts to feel the pain of letting go. I must replace my empty rooms, so I choose the furniture of joy, love, and peace. I now hear knocking at my door a host of my beautiful promises. I am excited to entertain my blissful company of delight; oh, it feels so good having faith and patience holding my hand while love smells up my fabulous being with prophetic whispers of truth.

Thank you, God, of the Highest!

☙ Chapter 16 ☙

Imagine Me

(Imagine Me Song Artist Kirk Franklin)

*"And the very God of peace sanctify you wholly; and I pray
God your whole spirit and soul and body be preserved
blameless unto the coming of our Lord Jesus Christ.*

1 Thessalonians 5:23 (KJV)

RELIGIOUS SHACKLES CHALLENGE: YOUR THREE MINDS

Many famous spiritual mystics and wisdom speakers spoke of the two minds: consciousness and subconsciousness. Unfortunately, religious leaders that are held by religious shackles are ignorant of your spiritual mind. Religious shackles (bonds) want to keep your mind in a state of ignorance, relying only on your physical senses to guide you throughout life and not by faith. It wants to open the door to you for a world of diseases while closing the door to the Kingdom of God.

I have proven success with my clients using the two-mind concept. However, my revelation furthers the concept to three minds: conscious, subconscious, and God-conscious. Conscious is me I see in the mirror. Subconscious is me that is invisible. God-conscious is my I am-ness.

Conscious Mind	Subconscious Mind	God-Conscious Mind
Me	Myself	I
Male	Female	I Am
Physical	Spiritual	Kingdom of God
Visible	Invisible	Garden of Eden
Words	Seeds	
Think	Vision	
Speech	Whisper	
Body	Soul	
Limited	Unlimited	
Temporary	Permanent	
Five Senses	Emotions	
Outward	Inward	
Effect	Cause	
Impress	Express	
Awake	Sleep	
Earth	Heaven	

Phyllis Y. Whitley

"Let this mind be in you which was also in Christ Jesus."

Philippians 2:5 (KJV)

SPIRITUAL SOVEREIGNTY SOLUTION: AGREEMENT

"Again, I say unto you, that if two of you shall agree on earth as touching anything that they shall ask, it shall be done for them of my Father which is in heaven."

Matthew 18:19 (KJV)

Inspection Time

Similarly, your conscious mind is your own traffic controller, examining and directing what you allow into your five lanes (gates) called *sight, smell, hearing, taste,* and *touch.* Religious shackles will keep you walking by your five senses, but God said you must walk by faith, not by sight *(2 Corinthians 5:7).* The beauty of your vehicle might get people's attention, but what is inside the hood is what will pass inspection. Yes, it is a necessity to take care of your covering (conscious mind). Still, it is even more crucial to take care of your inside parts (subconscious mind) with proper tune-ups (the word) and oil changes (emotions) according to your specific vehicle owner's manual (God-conscious mind).

When you want to know how to take care of and learn about your specific vehicle, you usually read your owner's manual. In the same way, when you want to know how to take care of and learn about your two minds, examine first the kingdom of God within you (God-conscious) unless you want to end up on the side of the road with a rejection sticker.

Corporate Order

Your conscious mind is like a supervisor who oversees your lower (physical) self that receives all thoughts, ideas, words, and inner whispers through your five-senses gate. Your subconscious mind is your executive who carries out the plans of your conscious mind. She is your spiritual self that waits until the midnight hour for your consciousness to enter her garden of Eden (mind) during *sleep, visualization, affirmation, or prayer*. She awaits his daily performance report, whether it is good or bad. Your God Conscious mind is the governor who controls your spirit within (kingdom of God). This is where the supernatural meets miracles and is activated once all minds agree to your spiritual contract.

> *"Examine yourselves, whether ye be in the faith; prove your own selves. Know ye not your own selves, how that Jesus Christ is in you, except ye be reprobates?"*
>
> 2 Corinthians 13:5 (KJV)

Spiritual Sovereignty Action

Examine your mind's contract daily so it will agree together.

SELF-WHISPER EXERCISE

1. What "me" do you see in the mirror?

2. Do you guide what goes into your subconscious mind? Why do you have to guide what goes into your subconscious mind?

3. What activities can you perform that will connect to your subconscious mind?

MEDITATION QUOTES

"Your conscious mindset sets the tone; your subconscious mind writes it in stone."

Phyllis Y. Whitley

"As you sow in your subconscious mind, so shall you reap in your body and environment."

Joseph Murphy

MEDITATION THERAPY

Every night and some days, I await Your love into my garden with rich seeds that I can soak up and cultivate. Then, I hand it to my Father God, who will make it visible so that our secret will be revealed. I trust that You, Father God, will bring the best seeds that will manifest into greatness where I can showcase them on my world stage play called my promised land.

☙ Chapter 17 ☙

The Secret Garden

(The Secret Garden Song Artist Quincy Jones)

"And they twain shall be one flesh: so then they are no more twain, but one flesh."

Mark 10:8 (KJV)

RELIGIOUS SHACKLES CHALLENGE: HUSBAND AND WIFE

Your conscious is the husband that goes unto his wife (subconscious) during sleep with all his worldly seeds (words, thoughts, whispers) that came from the five senses he collected throughout his awaken hours from other people, places, and things. The wife's womb will accept the husband's seeds with an agreement and loving persuasiveness without question, regardless of whether they are good or bad seeds.

As the two, not three or more of them, become one flesh, only some of his seeds will survive in her womb. The seeds of emotions that traveled and brought her to a climax will manifest as their children (life issues) from her garden of Eden, into your visible, physical world, creating your reality as heaven or hell. However, religious shackles will cause you to overfeed your flesh and ignore your spirit allowing your flesh to overtake it. Overfeeding your flesh and underfeeding your spirit will cause your flesh to become greedy and crave additional people or things, resulting in an uncontrollable addiction

"Whom I shall see for myself, and mine eyes shall behold, and not another; though my reins be consumed within me."

Job 19:27 KJV)

SPIRITUAL SOVEREIGNTY SOLUTION: GAME CONTROL

Computer Game

There are some basic computer operations types: Inputting, processing, outputting, storing, and printing. **Spiritual sovereignty** minds are like computers. Your conscious mind inputs what your five senses give it, and then your subconscious will start processing all data (ideas, words, whispers) that come to it with an attachment of emotions. Only the most dominant emotions are stored, and your superior God-conscious mind will control the way your data is printed on your world stage. In other words, it's very crucial what you put into your conscious mind because your subconscious mind can't take a joke, so she will process any repeated words or thoughts that have strong emotions.

Remember that God will give you the desires of your heart, good or bad, so don't be surprised when your world seems upside down because no one told you how to discipline your mind. If your world needs to change, consider taking back your game controller and giving it to God.

"Now I beseech you, brethren, by the name of our Lord Jesus Christ, that ye all speak the same thing, and that there be no divisions among you; but that ye be perfectly joined together in the same mind and in the same judgment."

1 Corinthians 1:10 (KJV)

Spiritual Sovereignty Action

Operate your minds to the ultimate version of you.

SELF-WHISPER EXERCISE

1. Are your addictions taking over your life?

2. Do you feel in control of your emotions?

3. What horror game is playing in your life?

MEDITATION QUOTES

"Your subconscious mind rides on your emotions."

Phyllis Y. Whitley

"Act the way you want to be and soon you'll be the way you act."

Les Brown

MEDITATION THERAPY

As I look in my mirror, I see a **virtuous beauty** called
me.My body is a magnificent, developing sculpture.
I love my skin, shade, and texture; oh, how beautiful it shows on me.
Even my scars are my secret meanings revealing the uniqueness of
me.
I smell so good, just like the flower that is really me.
I enjoy giving my skin what it needs as it talks to me.
Oh, how exquisite is my touch!
I choose who can share that special journey with me.
My tattoos are my **silent whispers** beneath my skin.
My smile is my candlelight in me.
My laughter is my medicine within.
My speech is full of sweet rhythms in me.
My eyes are mirroring my soul from
within.
My Father God is my true **divinity** in me.
Thank you, Father God, for revealing you **within** me!

☙ Chapter 18 ☙

Under New Management

(Under New Management Song Artist Miki Howard)

"Let the Lord, the God of the spirits of all flesh, set a man over the congregation."

Numbers 27:16.

RELIGIOUS SHACKLES CHALLENGE: FALSE PROPHET

Religious shackles are spirits that many people call *Lucifer, devil, Satan,* or whatever you choose to call them. Remember, you usually call out one name when life issues come, but what you don't realize is that you receive what you name it because your subconscious and God-conscious mind will give it to you in the form of manifestation.

The Bible is God's world play with different characters playing out their roles. Each character is playing a true prophet or false prophet with different names that are spirits in your mind today. When you choose the helmet of salvation, you choose the Holy Spirit and Jesus Christ, and this will set a watch over your mind (congregation). Consequently, if you do not choose a prophet (spirit), then the world will most likely select the false prophets (Lucifer, devil, Satan) for you. Therefore, God told us not to be double-minded because you are either a false prophet or a true prophet of God.

"He is a double-minded man, unstable in all his ways."

James 1:8 (NKJV)

SPIRITUAL SOVEREIGNTY SOLUTION: PROPHET WITHIN

When you put on your helmet of salvation, your spirit mind will go through life cycles that will lead you to your stage play, whether Prophet Daniel is playing a conqueror defeating your lion's den, or as King Solomon managing both your wisdom and wealth accordingly. How about Prophetess Esther, who stood in the gap for her family and community?

The spiritual sovereignty mind knows how to play several true prophets' roles by choosing the right prophetic spirits to receive while keeping out the false prophetic spirits. You must feed the prophet within you with soul food daily, or you might be feeding a false spirit, and we know what happens when you feed hell. You reap havoc on your stage play called the "The Kingdom of Hell." Choose to let the true prophet in you to speak through you and to you.

I will raise up for them a Prophet like you from among their brethren, and will put My words in His mouth, and He shall speak to them all that I command Him.

Deuteronomy 18:18 (NKJV)

Spiritual Sovereignty Action

Allow the prophet in you to speak God's Words.

SELF-WHISPER EXERCISE

1. Are what you say and what you are experiencing one in the same?

2. Does what you feel and think match with what you say?

3. Have you found the real prophet inside of you?

4. Do you know who to prophesy to yourself? If so, How?

MEDITATION QUOTES

"Prophesying to your self is your silent whispers brought to light."

Phyllis Y. Whitley

"We are the ones we've been waiting for."

Barack Obama

MEDITATION THERAPY

As I lay down to sleep, my garden of Eden is secretly developing my inward vision of prosperity, fulfilling my like-minded mate into my life story now. It is done, Father!

Today and every day, my mind is downloading nothing but the best for my family and me, as we prosper coming in and going out. Thank you, my Brilliant Lord!

All my minds are on one accord manifesting my heart's desire of peace, joy, love, and laughter at this present moment. Thanks, Infinite God within!

I am receiving smooth flowing traffic of people, places, and things into my life right now on my beautiful stage of life; forever, giving.

Thank you, my Immeasurable God.

☙ Chapter 19 ☙

Mark My Words

(Mark My Words Song Artist Eminem)

*"So shall my word be that goeth forth out of my mouth: it
shall not return unto me void, but it shall accomplish that
which I please, and it shall prosper in the thing whereto I
sent it."*

Isaiah 55:11 (KJV)

RELIGIOUS SHACKLES CHALLENGE: YOUR MOUTH

Religious shackles leaders are robbing you of your true power
because they want you to continue to depend on your flesh side,
causing you to be led blindly by your five senses. Are you listening
and watching people, places, and things that lift you or tear you down;
make you feel angry or happy; cause you to love or hurt, or cause you
to depress or impress? Religious shackle leaders fall short every time
with the above scripture because God is not only referring to Himself,
but He is also referring to you.

Yes! Your word will not fall to the ground because the word is
spirit, and spirit travels near and far using no transportation to deliver
your word back to you. Be careful not to use your words lightly, or it
will become a spell cast. This is why Jesus said to bless those who
mistreat you because he knows how your word would turn into curses
bouncing back to you. Become selective of what goes into your

conscious mind and absorbs deep into your subconscious mind. It will soon turn into words that might hurt you or help you today and tomorrow, so don't be so quick to want revenge on your enemies, or you will see it all fulfilled and manifested on your life's stage.

SPIRITUAL SOVEREIGNTY SOLUTION: MOUTHWASH

In the beginning, God spoke the word and then saw that it was good. He made sure both of them were in agreement. Spiritual sovereignty is first learning how to discipline what you think about all day long, including what you read, watch, and hear around you. Don't worry about all the negativity that goes on in this world. Start to guide your conscious mind and become mindful of what and who triggers your emotions so your life will not turn into a road of rages and fatal unhappiness. Instead, embrace sovereignty therapy by feeding your mind soul food and washing your words with love so that your mind and mouth will be in agreement. This is so important to hold on to since your subconscious and God-conscious never sleep but are ready to heal, solve, revise, and travel beyond your imagination so all your heart's desires will manifest and not return unto you void *(Genesis 1)*.

"Now you shall speak to him and put the words in his mouth. And I will be with your mouth and with his mouth, and I will teach you what you shall do."

Exodus 4:15 (NKJV)

Spiritual Sovereignty Action

Become mindful of what and who triggers your emotions.

SELF-WHISPER EXERCISE

1. What has been triggering your emotions?

2. What can you feed into your subconscious mind to turn your situation around?

3. How can you wash out the words in your mouth?

4. Why is it essential for your mouth and mind to line up?

MEDITATION QUOTES

"I don't curse people out; I bless them in."

Phyllis Y. Whitley

"Turn your wounds into wisdom."

Oprah Winfrey

MEDITATION THERAPY

I abide in God's Word today.
I have decided to meditate on God's word throughout my day.
I forgive and let go of all my limitations today.
Therefore, no lack, curse, voodoo spell, or negative words can enter my house today.
Both my spiritual and physical houses are blessed today.
Thank you, God, for overseeing my castle today!

❦ Chapter 20 ❦

Boulevard of Broken Dream

(Boulevard of Broken Dream Song Artist Green Day)

"And Joseph dreamed a dream, and he told it to his brethren: and they hated him yet the more."

Genesis 37:5

RELIGIOUS SHACKLES CHALLENGE: DREAM TERMINATOR

Religious shackles tried to terminate Joseph's dreams and words through his brothers' jealousy before it could be fulfilled. Likewise, this same spirit wants to stop and abort your dreams today, causing you to live a life of unfulfilled dreams. Let's look at the fact that the Wright Brothers' airplane was a daydream first that went from their invisible to our visible world. With strong beliefs and a persistent dream, the first airplane was made flesh. Likewise, Thomas Edison's light bulb was also a dream that became flesh. How can you make your dreams a reality?

The Wright Brothers did not see a half of a plane, nor did Edison see a piece of a light bulb. They were persistent through all their failed tests and many criticisms. Fear not when people laugh at your dreams. Past and present inventors were laughed at and mocked also. Can you imagine what a black inventor of the 20th century named George Washington Carver went through before his dreams came to fruition?

I am sure he overlooked and mocked too, but Mr. Carver continued inventing numerous edible and non-food products from sweet potatoes and peanuts.

Did you ever think about what your life would be like without your telephone? Remember that Alexander Graham Bell invented the first telephone causing many to believe he was crazy, including other inventors. How about another dream that made history? A man who became the first black president of the United States. Yes, many black men might have had this dream, but only one man named Barack Obama pushed his dream into a reality. Take your daydreams back, and do not be so quick to share it openly with everyone, or your dreams might wound up in the pit just like Joseph.

"So it came to pass, when Joseph had come to his brothers,
that they stripped Joseph of his tunic, the tunic of many
colors that was on him. Then they took him and cast him into
a pit. And the pit was empty; there was no water in it."

Genesis 37:23-24

SPIRITUAL SOVEREIGNTY SOLUTION: BLOCKBUSTER MOVIE

"And Pharaoh said unto Joseph, See, I have set thee over all
the land of Egypt...

And he made him to ride in the second chariot which he had;
and they cried before him, Bow the knee: and he made him
ruler over all the land of Egypt."

Genesis 41:41, 43(KJV)

Am I Dreaming?

Dreams come in two stages: (1) daydreams that are short occurring during meditation or visualization, and (2) night dreams that occur during sleeping hours. Your daydreams are movie trailers to God, and your night dreams are God's movie trailers to you. It should start making sense why you cannot share your dreams with everyone, even with your loved ones, because they do not know the whole movie; therefore, they will try to direct, even produce it.

Joseph's brothers threw him in the pit because they couldn't see that Joseph was a superstar, so they sought to abort his dreams, but because God knew the movie's ending, He was able to turn the brothers' mess into a blessing for everyone at the end.

Spiritual sovereignty is taking your eyes off your pit and putting it on your blockbuster movie. Stop waiting for God to come down and daydream for you! Use your meditation time to visualize daily to cast, direct, produce, and revise your movie trailer. This is your way of communicating to God until each of your dreams are released to your world screen. Watch God send back your finalized blockbuster picture with a note signed, "it's fulfilled!"

> *"At Gibeon the Lord appeared to Solomon in a dream by night; and God said, "Ask! What shall I give you?"*
>
> *1 Kings 3:5 (NKJV)*

Spiritual Sovereignty Action

Imagine your promise land with action behind it.

SELF-WHISPER EXERCISE

1. Where have you allowed failure to delay your dreams?

2. What dreams have you placed on a shelf from fear of rejection and ridicule?

3. What dreams would you fulfill if you had nothing to fear?

4. How many people do you know that took their dreams to their grave?

MEDITATION QUOTES

"Your daydreams are movie trailers to God, and your night dreams are God's movie trailers to you."

"Dream your blockbuster movie within until God releases it to the world."

Phyllis Y. Whitley

"You can kill the dreamer, but you can't kill the dream."

Martin Luther King, Jr.

MEDITATION THERAPY

My I AM-NESS

— Who am I? I Am your pre-views

— Who am I? I Am your dreams
— Who am I? I Am your advertisement
— Who am I? I Am heart desires
— Who am I? I Am your daytime snapshots
— Who am I? I Am you night movie trailer
— Who am I? I Am your blueprints
— Who am I? I Am your life script play
— Who am I? I Am your God
— Who am I? I Am you

☙ Chapter 21 ☙

Help! I've Been Robbed

(Love Robbery Song Artist Kalin and Myles)

"And with him they crucify two thieves; the one on his right hand, and the other on his left."

Mark 15:27 (KJV)

RELIGIOUS SHACKLES CHALLENGE: YOUR THIEVES

The two thieves that were crucified with Jesus represent your past and your future thieves. Jesus is your now, and the two thieves are fighting for your attention so you cannot enjoy your abundant life *now*. Religious shackles thrive on old traditions to keep you looking at your past losses, lack, regrets, and pain, so your present walk will be delayed or stopped altogether.

Religious shackles also do not want to see you prosper, so they tell you to live in a wanting stage now so God can give you the rest in Heaven. For this reason, religious rulers were angry with Jesus's immediate manifesting. You cannot be productive or advancing if you are stuck in your past or worrying about the how in your future.

SPIRITUAL SOVEREIGNTY SOLUTION: REVISION

"The thief cometh not, but for to steal, and to kill, and to destroy: I am come that they might have life, and that they might have it more abundantly."

John 10:10 (KJV)

Memories

It does not take a rocket scientist to know that you must let go of your past, stay focused on God's present, and stop agonizing about tomorrow. Was it not strange that the Pharisees were always telling Jesus how he could not do this or that while all along, Jesus's actions were fulfilling the Old Testament's prophecies? God does not want you to look back at your past or worry about your tomorrow. Your past and future can only be reviewed, revisited, and revised from within you. Today is your only conscious actuality. Besides, today is the only time you can "take action." Yesterday can be your revision, and tomorrow can only be your reaction today.

"Therefore do not worry about tomorrow, for tomorrow will worry about itself."

Matthew 6:34 (NIV).

Spiritual Sovereignty Action

Live in your present, and revise your past to change your future.

SELF-WHISPER EXERCISE

1. Are you allowing your past to dictate your present identity?

2. What actions are you taking now to become your greatest self?

3. Where are you stuck at, and how can you change your actions moving forward?

MEDITATION QUOTES

"Yesterday can be your revision, and tomorrow can only be your reaction for today."

"If you stop producing fruit, then God will stop producing for you."

Phyllis Y. Whitley

"Where there is no vision, there is no hope."

George Washington Carver

MEDITATION THERAPY

To everything, there is a season:

- A time for every purpose under heaven: I am thankful for preparation.
- A time to be born: I am being renewed daily.
- A time to die: I am letting go of my past pain.
- A time to plant: I am sowing good seed daily.

- A time to pluck what is planted: I am removing all negative people, places, and things from my life.
- A time to kill: I am releasing the old me daily.
- A time to heal: my heart forgives my enemies.
- A time to break down: I fell yesterday but I got back up today.
- A time to build up: God lifts me up daily.
- A time to weep: God is wiping my past tears.
- A time to laugh: laughter is my daily medicine.
- A time to mourn: I miss you, but I must move on.
- And a time to dance: I am rejoicing in my promise land.

Ecclesiastes 3:1-4

☙ Chapter 22 ☙

Back Down Memory Lane

(Back Down Memory Lane Song Artist Minnie Riperton)

"But Lot's wife looked back, and she became a pillar of salt."

Genesis 19:26 (NIV)

RELIGIOUS SHACKLES CHALLENGE: YOUR FUTURE/PAST THIEF

Religious shackles can come as your future thief putting things off until tomorrow when your tomorrow never comes. This thief will have you procrastinating about some things, being lazy most of the time, making excuses anytime, complaining about everything, and worrying always.

The future thief kills your today, so you become fearful of the what-ifs. The future thief also brings you the box called fear of rejection that blinds you during life issues such as divorce or being fired from your job, causing you to believe that there is no hope for tomorrow. Instead of feeling and seeing only the end of your situation, start to see the beginning of something new. See yourself starting your own business. After a divorce, see yourself welcoming a transformation to the new you. Move on with your life and fall in love with yourself. There, you might be shocked to find God carrying you through your moment of crisis.

Likewise, religious shackles can come as your past thief bringing regrets or even traumatization to a point where it can cause suicidal thoughts or self-inflicted illnesses. Those old religious spirits want you to believe that you are flesh only with no spiritual side; but, when you realize your spirit has no end, then maybe you will think twice about death, killing, and even suicide. Your spirit is eternal.

Try this. Close your eyes and remember your last conversation or action shared with a deceased loved one. Now open your eyes. Where are they? Can you touch them? No! Yet, you could see and even hear them because another realm called the invisible spiritual realm is forever lasting.

SPIRITUAL SOVEREIGNTY SOLUTION: CELEBRATE

"And God shall wipe away all tears from their eyes; and there shall be no more death, neither sorrow, nor crying, neither shall there be any more pain: for the former things are passed away."

Revelation 21:4 (KJV)

How Can You Mend a Broken Heart?

Death is the ending of your flesh but the beginning of your deceased one's heavenly life with Jehovah God. So, hold on to this, and you will learn to cherish your memories, knowing you two will be together again in spirit. Knowing this truth will not stop your grieving, but now you understand that all fleshly bodies must go back to dust while every spirit moves to eternity.

There are things you can do to celebrate a loved one's life on this earth; have a memorial of his or her favorite (sport, color, movie, hobby, or work, etc.). You can celebrate his or her birthday by doing something fun. You can join an online group that shares the same interest or start a nonprofit organization in their name to help others.

The real revelation is that your deceased loved one got the better deal while you are still trying to find your internal God within. They are rejoicing in a realm called everlasting with the Almighty God.

A merry heart does good, like medicine, but a broken spirit dries the bones.

Proverbs 17:22 (NKJV)

Spiritual Sovereignty Action

Release past pain while embracing your new season.

SELF-WHISPER EXERCISE

1. Can you embrace your present without fear of the future?

2. Who or what are you holding on to?

3. Do you need help in letting go of past pain?

4. What kind of memorial can you start today to celebrate your loved one in honor?

MEDITATION QUOTES

"Be careful not to stay stuck in grief, or else people will be grieving for you sooner than later."

Phyllis Y. Whitley

"It's not the load that breaks you down, it's the way you carry it."

Lena Horne

"I forgive everyone in my past for all perceived wrongs, I release them with love."

Louise Hay

MEDITATION THERAPY

This Morning:

I open up my conscious awareness to my hearts' desire.
I open up my conscious thoughts to my desired visions.
I open up my conscious heart to receive more knowledge.
I open up my intelligent mind to perceive what's about to happen to me.
I open up my spiritual ears to hear only what healthy for me.
I open up my spiritual eyes to see what God sees for me.
I open up my mouth to prophesies truth to me and others.
I open up my fabulous future from today.
Oh, how I praise you, Lord, for all the new opportunities opening up for me today!

☙ Chapter 23 ☙

My Seed

(Letter 2 My First Seed Song Artist Six Pound)

*"Then God blessed them, and God said to them, "Be fruitful
and multiply; fill the earth and subdue it... And God said,
"See, I have given you every herb that yields seed which is
on the face of all the earth, and every tree whose fruit yields
seed; to you it shall be for food."*

Genesis 1:28-29 (NKJV)

RELIGIOUS SHACKLES CHALLENGE: MISPLACED SEED

Religious shackles want God's seed – *you*. In the beginning, was
the word (seed), and out of His word, He created you from His
thoughts (imagination), and He made you in His image (likeness).
Your purpose is to sow your seed properly to produce a harvest after
its own kind as it also continues to multiply. Therefore, God wants
you to be fruitful, unlike the first rebellious spirit Lucifer (devil), who
was cut off and now seedless. So now you know why he is roaming
the earth. The devil wants your seed because he has no seed. Since
he cannot reproduce, he must get in your garden and corrupt and stop
your generation's productivity, your dreams, and your visions. He is
a seed killer. Religion can keep you seedless since it plants everything
on the outside. How can you plant on the outside of a garden or pot?
You can't.

"For he, that soweth to his flesh shall of the flesh reap corruption; but he that soweth to the Spirit shall of the Spirit reap life everlasting."

Galatians 6:8 (KJV)

Why do you think there are more women than men in the church? No fathers in the home? Why are women barren, aborting, and miscarrying? It is because of the seed they carry. It has become the norm of this generation for men to misuse or misplace their seeds and keep it out of a garden to only spill his seed in a soil-less field.

The same can be said for women to desire a seedless handmade male organ instead of a man. To go deeper, many married and single men are on the down-low, giving their seed to both fertile soil and infertile soil, which have caused a host of chaos, STDs, diseases, and shame. God is forgiving, and He loves all His creations, but He wants order with the seed. He knows that if His laws are not followed, then His body (the universe) will bring the consequences to your feet as He did with Sodom and Gomorrah.

"For this reason, God gave them up to vile passions. For even their women exchanged the natural use for what is against nature. Likewise also the men, leaving the natural use of the woman, burned in their lust for one another, men with men committing what is shameful, and receiving in themselves the penalty of their error which was due."

Romans 1:26-27 (NKJV)

SPIRITUAL SOVEREIGNTY SOLUTION: PLANT PROPERLY

"Now may He who supplies seed to the sower, and bread for food, supply and multiply the seed you have sown and increase the fruits of your righteousness, while you are enriched in everything for all liberality, which causes thanksgiving through us to God."

2 Corinthians 9:10-11 (NKJV)

Spiritual sovereignty souls understand the power of God's seeds whether we are talking about the seeds in food, in a male's semen, in a woman's womb, or even the seed in your mind. All must be cultivated and not misplaced. Being seeds, your thoughts are under attack by the world stage every day, so keep a watch on what comes into your five senses gates. Know why Jesus walked past the fig tree and cursed it. It was not producing fruit. Jesus even mentions how the man had his talent (money) taken away because he did not invest it but hid it away. God made you to be fruitful with your mind, body, and spirit. The true revelation here is to plant your seeds properly, or they will return unto you as weeds that choke God's real purpose for you. That is to multiply your greatness into your next generations.

"Therefore, I say to you, the kingdom of God will be taken from you and given to a nation bearing the fruits of it."

Matthew 21:43 (NKJV).

Spiritual Sovereignty Action

Plant your seeds according to God's words so your harvest will be great.

SELF-WHISPER EXERCISE

1. Have your seeds been sown in good grounds for manifestation?

2. Are you producing in all areas of your life according to God's decree?

3. In what area of your life have you stunted growth for future generations?

4. Have you or someone you know misplaced their seed? What was their consequence?

MEDITATION QUOTES

"Religion keeps you seedless because it plants everything on the outside."

"A real man plants his seeds on fertile ground. A foolish man scatters his seeds in every town."

"Seedless people produce only copycats and not originalities."

Phyllis Y. Whitley

MEDITATION THERAPY

Tonight, before I enter unto sleep, I choose to sow good seeds I received today.
My conscious mind is planting my seeds tonight.

My subconscious mind is working 24/7 to manifest it while I sleep. My God-conscious is making sure my seed will not return unto me empty.

Tomorrow, my seed will be revealed.

Thank you, angels, for bringing my abundant harvest while I lay down to go to sleep.

☙ Chapter 24 ❧

Distant Lover

(Distant Lover Song Artist Marvin Gaye)

"You shall not go after other gods, the gods of the peoples who are all around you (for the Lord your God is a jealous God among you), lest the anger of the Lord your God be aroused against you and destroy you from the face of the earth."

Deuteronomy 6:14-15 (NKJV)

RELIGIOUS SHACKLES CHALLENGE: OTHER GODS

You whisper to yourself, "I don't serve other gods," or "how can I serve other gods when I am in church every time the doors open?" Unfortunately, you forgot about the people and things outside you that you meditate on and serve each day. In some cases, you are addicted to these things, your boyfriend or girlfriend, your friends and family, your husband or wife, food, alcohol, gambling, drugs, medication, sex, phone, computer, social media, idols, or yourself.

Yes! These are your hidden religious shackles. However, churches are not speaking about this because some leaders are blinded or are addicted themselves. You whisper to your boyfriend or girlfriend, "I can't live without you" or, to your mate, "I'll die if I can't have you." You whisper to your food, "I can't get enough of you when I am stressed," or, "I can't stop eating my favorite…" or, "I am glad no one sees me eating this, especially at night." You whisper to your alcohol and drugs, "I spent my last dollar to have you" or, "you make me feel so good." You whisper to your flesh, "I just can't get enough sex; I don't know what's wrong with me" or, "I'll sleep with anybody right now because I am so horny, " or "Give me my phone, I can't go a day without it."

Remember when you last stalked your former exes? How about when you stopped working to follow your favorite artist around the world? Have you stayed around your family or friends even though they put you down? Or maybe, when your loved one died, and you gave up your whole life because you could not live anymore? Are you serving money and owing everyone, having your money manage you instead of the other way around? Am I speaking to you? You are worshipping what is outside of you. Your attention is focused, meditated, on these things. You spend all your free time with everyone but God. Yes! God is Jealous.

"for you shall worship no other god, for the Lord, whose name is Jealous, is a jealous God."

Exodus 34:14 (NKJV)

SPIRITUAL SOVEREIGNTY SOLUTION: OUTSIDE DISCIPLINE

"Flee sexual immorality. Every sin that a man does is outside the body, but he who commits sexual immorality sins against his own body."

1 Corinthians. 6:18 (NKJV)

Greatest Love of All

God is jealous, but He is also a forgiving God. Spiritual sovereignty knows the truth about all these addictions. First, you do not love yourself, so you seek outside of you to find peace and love to fulfill the void you have had from a child. Secondly, your flesh is undisciplined, and your spirit needs therapy so it can keep your flesh in check. When you search within, you will find God, despite your religious shackles' lies. If you are suffering from a bad addiction, check to see if you are overfeeding your flesh and starving your spirit. Put no trust in your flesh, or you will find yourself doing everything and anything to please it, so remember that it has an ending. Consistently feeding your spirit will yield you the Kingdom of God within since your spirit will be strong enough to keep your flesh in check.

"For all that is in the world—the lust of the flesh, the lust of the eyes, and the pride of life—is not of the Father but is of the world."

1 John 2:16 (NKJV)

Spiritual Sovereignty Action

Worship and love only God within while releasing all your other gods.

SELF-WHISPER EXERCISE

1. What everyday habits have you made your god?

2. What steps can you take to discipline your flesh?

3. How are you feeding your spirit the correct way?

MEDITATION QUOTES

"The power is not in all the outside things you worship; it's within."

Phyllis Y. Whitley

"Your inner being is he who men call God."

Neville Goddard

"Yes, if you'll but seek Me thus, making Me first in your life, never resting until you do find Me, it won't be long before you'll become conscious of My Presence, of My Loving Voice, speaking constantly from out the depths of your heart."

Joseph S. Benner

MEDITATION THERAPY

Every time I let you go, you seem to come right back to me with uninvited guests. I recognize your friend's idolatry, drunkenness, and promiscuity waiting for an opportunity to be invited into my home. I will never forget how dissensions tried to come into my house and take over, but not anymore. I meant to ask you why your cousin gluttony follows me wherever I go; especially, when dining out.

This has been going on too long, and you must tell your twin couples of sexual immorality and moral impurity to stop trying to come through my gate at night. They are not welcomed here. Do not forget to tell the triplets depression, anger, and selfishness that I changed the locks on my door so they can stop waiting at my steps.

Now that I realize you were never a real friend because you loved talking about me to jealousy and envy behind my back; therefore, I release you out of my life.

I have a new landlord, named Jesus Christ! I am under a new contract with faith, and I welcome my new tenants named joy, love, and patience. Self-control, meekness, and temperance are also my new maintenance crew. I asked goodness, gentleness, and kindness to guide my house forever. Although most of us are hidden, do not be fooled, we see and hear everything.

I am laughing my way to freedom.

ꙮ Chapter 25 ꙮ

Home

(Home Song Artist Stephanie Mills)

"And not many days after, the younger son gathered all together, journeyed to a far country, and there wasted his possessions with prodigal living."

Luke 15:13 (NKJV)

RELIGIOUS SHACKLES CHALLENGE: THE LOST

This chapter is about a rich man's son who took his wealth and left home to a faraway country. The prodigal son misspent his riches until he was poor and found himself at his lowest job ever, cleaning pigs. He then came to himself. He whispered to himself what he would say to his father upon his return because, at that moment, he had made up in his mind that the grass was not greener on the other side. He went to his father to try to get back in, but long before he arrived home, his father saw him and ran to him. Although the prodigal son was humbled enough to take a lower position as the hired help, his father said no and instead brought out the best garments, food, and drinks to celebrate his son's return home. The eldest son was jealous of how his younger brother was being treated despite having left. The father explained that he was happy for both sons; however, he said his youngest son was dead and lost. Now that his son had returned to him, he is considered alive and no longer lost. In other words, his youngest son was no longer under the influence of religious shackles that had him trusting in his outside world.

> *"It was right that we should make merry and be glad, for your brother was dead and is alive again, and was lost and is found."*

> *Luke 15:32 (NKJV)*

SPIRITUAL SOVEREIGNTY SOLUTION: FINDING YOURSELF

> *"But seek ye first the kingdom of God, and his righteousness; and all these things shall be added unto you."*

> *Matthew 6:33 (KJV)*

Home

The prodigal son is *you*. When you traveled away from God to seek Him on the outside of you, God was right there waiting for you to come to your spiritual senses by realizing that the kingdom of God is within you. Never mind those who get jealous. God loves everyone because everybody is Him, pushed out. If you faithfully read this whole book, then you are home, and you are ready to live the spiritually sovereign life as you let go of those old religious chains. Be coachable. Be forever a student and embrace spiritual therapy so you can feed your spirit soul food daily. Live like you are already your desires. Learn to prophesy to yourself. Write your desired life play in your mind, dream, visualize, affirm, and get ready to manifest all your wonderful desires in your outer world through your inner self (God). In due season your word will not fall to the ground but will show you your revised life stage play called your promised land. Welcome home, prodigal sons and daughters!

"Neither shall they say, lo here! or, lo there! for, behold, the kingdom of God is within you. "

Luke 17:21(KJV)

Spiritual Sovereignty Action

Discard your old religious life play and write your new life's play until it's fulfilled, and you too can say, like Jesus said, "it is Finished!"

"After this, Jesus, knowing that all things were now accomplished, that the Scripture might be fulfilled, said, "I thirst!" Now a vessel full of sour wine was sitting there; and they filled a sponge with sour wine, put it on hyssop, and put it in His mouth. So when Jesus had received the sour wine, He said, "It is finished!" And bowing His head, He gave up His spirit. "

John 19:28-30 (NKJV)

SELF-WHISPER EXERCISE

1. Have you stopped looking towards the world to find your real purpose?

2. Have you realized that only God knows your true purpose, and that answer resides within you?

3. Are you ready to stop seeking God outside of you?

4. Are you ready to write your new life play? Why?

MEDITATION QUOTES

"The prodigal son or daughter will eventually come to his/her senses, but a fool has no common senses."

"Great whispers will manifest your extraordinary life play; bad whispers will manifest payless reruns."

"God is the producer of your life play, and you are the writer, director, and actor. Fire your old self and rewrite your life play."

Phyllis Y. Whitley

MEDITATION THERAPY

It's so good to be home again, in the house of the Lord, where I belong. I am no longer traveling to see God because God is with me and within me. This is the day God has made, and I will let my smile be a witness to all that I encounter today.

Conclusion

What do you do when you followed all your traditional religious protocols, and year after year, the only one who is prospering is your spiritual leader? No, it is not their job to take you by the hand and spoon feed you, but it is his or her job to feed you the good news (gospel) that will not only prosper your mind, body, and soul but will put you on the right road of your divine destiny with no harm done. *"Woe to the shepherds of Israel who feed themselves! Should not the shepherds feed the flocks? You eat the fat and clothe yourselves with the wool; you slaughter the fatlings, but you do not feed the flock"* *(Ezekiel 34:2-3, NKJV)*

Each chapter in this book gave you a preview of how bondage tried to take over Jesus and can easily take over a person's spirit. Likewise, each chapter gave you a spiritual solution and therapy you can use each day as you learn how to incorporate them into your new life play starring you. Not only will you experience milk and honey but also abundance in all areas of your life. Know that God is in both the beginning and end of your life's play waiting for you to manifest all your good desires by walking through the one and only door there is – Jesus. *"I am the Alpha and the Omega, the Beginning and the End,"* says the Lord, *"who is and who was and who is to come, the Almighty"(Revelation. 1:8, NKJV)*.

Forgive those spiritual leaders who misused or abuse you. Take off your religious shackles and embrace spiritual sovereignty as you continue to master and manifest your true kingdom riches from within. You could either continue to stay in lack and wait on the will of God or move and become the will of God. The choice is yours. *"I am the door. If anyone enters by Me, he will be saved, and will go in and out and find pasture,"(John 10:9, NKJV).*

"Stop believing in a God above the sky and start believing in a God within your mind."

Phyllis Y. Whitley

Dear Mama Dedication

"Honour thy father and thy mother: that thy days may be long upon the land which the Lord thy God giveth thee"

Exodus 20:12 (KJV)

She will keep you by choice. She will wipe your tears of pain, hunger, and sadness. She will stretch all household dollars for a rainy day. Yes! Some call her wonder woman. She will cover your mistakes and shame. She will love you even when you do not love her at times. Her availability is morning, noon, and night. Her laughter is your joy. She prayed for your success and health before you were grown. In summary, she is your first friend, first boss, first maid, first cook, first hairstylist, first teacher, first doctor, first lawyer, first banker, first security guard, first prayer warrior, first counselor, first prophetess, and first pastor.

Please recognize and reward her all the days of her life without judgment because you too will be standing alone at her homecoming, unable to turn the clock back but controlling your tears, whispering to yourself, "farewell, my angel." Simultaneously, everyone is perplexed at your endless smile that appreciates and believes that mother is in a better place, continuously praying on my behalf until we meet again at my homecoming.

Phyllis Y. Whitley

SELF-WHISPER POEM

A Homecoming Celebration

"O death, where is thy sting? O grave, where is thy victory?"

1 Corinthians. 15:55

Oh, New Orleans, you lost your religious shackles decades ago,
You now know the true revelation of death; death is an illusion.
No more long depression, forever goodbye, and anger at God's
funerals.
Whether your loved one died unexpectedly, tragically, accidentally,
or incurably.
Embrace your season to grieve the body,
Then trust that their spirit went to a better realm,
Naturally, mourn through your preparation for a celebration.
Meanwhile, everyone watches as you celebrate your loved one to
their last promotion.
You whisper to them, "don't forget to visit me in my dreams."
Or "whisper in my ear when I visit you in my mind's eyes."
Goodbye, my loved one… Until we meet again
Now put on your new body and get ready to meet the King of Kings,
Jesus Christ, our Lord.

SELF-WHISPER POEM
Remember Me!

I have been through the fiery furnace because God was breaking me
in five ways:

1. **Planning** – God had a plan for me to learn my true value
   through my own wilderness.

---

2. **Cleaving** – My selfish desires pulled and shaped me to God's desired vessel.
3. **Cutting** – My rough character had to be cut out by God so I can produce good fruit.
4. **Polishing** – God clothed me in righteousness and humility, and uniqueness.
5. **Inspection** – Before God called me, I had to meet His specifications to lead by example.

Remember me! I am who you lied on, who you backstabbed, who you were jealous of, who you abandoned, who you call stupid and ugly, who you said would never make it, who you called crazy, and who you laughed at and made fun of.

Now look at me closer, what do you see? A Diamond called me.

Meditation Scriptural Therapy

Then Isaac planted [seed] in that land [as a farmer] and reaped in the same year a hundred times [as much as he had planted], and the Lord blessed and favored him. (Genesis 26:12)

And all the tithe of the land, whether of the seed of the land, or of the fruit of the tree, is the Lord's: it is holy unto the Lord. (Leviticus 27:30)

I call heaven and earth to record this day against you, that I have set before your life and death, blessing, and cursing: therefore, choose life, that both thou and thy seed may live. (Deuteronomy. 30:19)

And when he saw a fig tree in the way, he came to it, and found nothing thereon, but leaves only, and said unto it, let no fruit grow on thee henceforward forever. And presently the fig tree withered away. (Matthew 21:19)

And God said, "See, I have given you every herb that yields seed which is on the face of all the earth, and every tree whose fruit yields seed; to you it shall be for food." (Genesis 1:29)

While the earth remains, Seedtime and harvest, Cold and heat, Winter and summer, and day and night Shall not cease. (Genesis 8:22)

In your seed all the nations of the earth shall be blessed, because you have obeyed My voice. (Genesis 22:18)

And I will make your descendants multiply as the stars of heaven; I will give to your descendants all these lands; and in your seed all the nations of the earth shall be blessed. (Genesis 26:4)

I also will do this to you: I will even appoint terror over you, wasting disease and fever which shall consume the eyes and cause sorrow of heart. And you shall sow your seed in vain, for your enemies shall eat it. (Leviticus 26:16).

And I will put enmity Between you and the woman, and between your seed and her Seed; He shall bruise your head, and you shall bruise His heel." (Genesis 3:15)

The fear of the Lord is the beginning of knowledge: but fools despise wisdom and instruction. (Proverbs 1:7)

Trust in the Lord with all thine heart; and lean not unto thine own understanding. (Proverbs 3:5).

The spirit of man is the candle of the Lord, searching all the inward parts of the belly (Proverbs 20:27)

All the ways of a man are clean in his own eyes; but the Lord weigheth the spirits. (Proverbs 16:2)

And there are three that bear witness in earth, the Spirit, and the water, and the blood: and these three agree in one. (1 John 5:8)

I am crucified with Christ: nevertheless I live; yet not I, but Christ liveth in me: and the life which I now live in the flesh I live by the faith of the Son of God, who loved me, and gave himself for me. (Galatians 2:20)

For God sent not his Son into the world to condemn the world; but that the world through him might be saved. (John 3:17)

For the kingdom of God is not based on talk but on power. (1 Corinthians 4:20)

In the beginning, was the Word, and the Word was with God, and the Word was God. (John 1:1)

All the ways of a man are clean in his own eyes; but the Lord weighed the spirits. (Proverbs 16:2)

Where there is no vision, the people perish: but he that keepeth the law, happy is he. (Proverbs 29:18)

Hold fast the form of sound words, which thou hast heard of me, in faith and love which is in Christ Jesus. That good thing which was committed unto thee keep by the Holy Ghost which dwelleth in us. (2 Timothy 1:13-14).

I thank God—through Jesus Christ our Lord! So then, with the mind I myself serve the law of God, but with the flesh the law of sin. (Romans 7:25)

Blessed be the God and Father of our Lord Jesus Christ, who has blessed us with every spiritual blessing in the heavenly places in Christ (Ephesians 1:3)

He who finds a wife finds a good thing and obtains favor from the Lord. (Proverbs 18:22)

And we have known and believed the love that God hath to us. God is love; and he that dwelleth in love dwelleth in God, and God in him. (1 John 4:16)

Death and life are in the power of the tongue: and they that love it shall eat the fruit thereof. (Proverbs 18:21)

If thou doest well, shalt thou no be accepted? and if thou doest not well, sin lieth at the door. And unto thee shall be his desire, and thou shalt rule over him. (Genesis 4:7)

Other gods Scriptural References:

And put a knife to your throat If you are a man given to appetite. Do not desire his delicacies, for they are deceptive food. (Proverbs 23:2-3)

Yet ye have forsaken me and served other gods: wherefore I will deliver you no more. (Judges 10:13)

And Jacob said to his household and to all who were with him, "Put away the foreign gods that are among you, purify yourselves, and change your garments. (Genesis 35:2)

Now I know that the Lord is greater than all the gods; for in the very thing in which they behaved proudly; He was above them. (Exodus 18:11)

You shall not bow down to their gods, nor serve them, nor do according to their works; but you shall utterly overthrow them and completely break down their sacred pillars. (Exodus 23:24)

Do not turn to idols, nor make for yourselves molded gods: I am the Lord your God. (Leviticus 19:4)

Being filled with all unrighteousness, sexual immorality, wickedness, covetousness, maliciousness; full of envy, murder, strife, deceit, evil-mindedness; they are whisperers. (Romans 1:29)

as Sodom and Gomorrah, and the cities around them in a similar manner to these, having given themselves over to sexual immorality and gone after strange flesh, are set forth as an example, suffering the vengeance of eternal fire. (Jude 1:7)

But the cowardly, unbelieving, abominable, murderers, sexually immoral, sorcerers, idolaters, and all liars shall have their part in the lake which burns with fire and brimstone, which is the second death. (Revelation 21:8)

No one can serve two masters; for either he will hate the one and love the other, or else he will be loyal to the one and despise the other. You cannot serve God and mammon. (Matthew 6:24)

8 Steps to Mastery & Manifesting Your Promised Land Within

1. Learn and study God's manuscript: *Study to shew thyself approved unto God, a workman that needeth not to be ashamed, rightly dividing the word of truth. (2 Timothy 2:15, KJV)*

2. Accept Jesus Christ as your Lord and savior from lack into your heart (spirit). *I am come that they might have life, and that they might have it more abundantly. (John 10:10, KJV)*

3. Receive God's gift of the Holy Spirit to guide your spiritual being. *But the Comforter, which is the Holy Ghost, whom the Father will send in my name, he shall teach you all things, and bring all things to your remembrance, whatsoever I have said unto you. (John 14:26, KJV)*

4. Worship God and feed your spirit within through meditation and affirmation. *Let the words of my mouth, and the meditation of my heart, be acceptable in thy sight, O Lord, my strength, and my redeemer. (Psalm 19:14, KJV)*

5. Worship God and feed your spirit within through prayers, fasting. *And he said unto them, this kind can come forth by nothing, but by prayer and fasting. (Mark 9:29) Watch and pray, that ye enter not into temptation: the spirit indeed is willing, but the flesh is weak. (Matthew 26:41, KJV)*

6. Honor God first with 10% of your first fruit. *Will a man rob God? Yet ye have robbed me. But ye say, wherein have we robbed thee? In tithes and offerings. (Malachi 3:8-10, KJV).*

7. Give generously by investing into who feed your spirit, to yourself and to the poor. *Give, and it shall be given unto you; good measure, pressed down, and shaken together, and running over, shall men give into your bosom. For with the same measure that ye mete withal it shall be measured to you again. (Luke 6:38, KJV).*

8. Fall in love with your God and his creations which includes you. *And thou shalt love the Lord thy God with all thine heart, and with all thy soul, and with all thy might. (Deut. 6:5, KJV). Neither shall they say, Lo here! or, lo there! for, behold, the kingdom of God is within you. (Luke 17:2, KJV).*

About the Author

Phyllis Y. Whitley was born and raised in Bronx, NY. She is the CEO and founder of Self Whisper, LLC and the nonprofit organization, WhisperVise. Phyllis graduated as a Certified Holistic Health Coach from the Institute for Integrative Nutrition. She is also a graduate of Liberty University with a Bachelor of Science in Psychology and Religion Studies and a Master of Arts in Human Service/Wellness.

Phyllis has gained the education, skills, and experiences of the empowerment and delivery of people from religious bondage and the lies that come with it. She is also an Ordained Minister who walks by God's truth, not her title.

Ever since her teens, Phyllis has been the go-to relationship guru. Over time, she discovered her passion for helping women in their relationship troubles that lead to relationship hurts. At the age of 26, Phyllis had given her life to Jesus Christ and began a personal discovery of another type of pain called Church Hurt. Additionally, she began wondering why so many men and women relishing in being gluttonous for punishment in their pain of self-hurt. Eventually, Phyllis had quickly learned that God desires to bless us holistically (mind, body, and soul) so we can do His work. *"Beloved, I pray that you may prosper in all things and be in health, just as your soul prospers." (3 John 1:2)*

A survivor of cancer, Phyllis has used her personal struggles and wisdom gained through past hurts to shape and mold her into the Queen Conscious being she is today. She has overcome many years of religious bondage and living a life full of lack. She now uses her own struggles to help guide others past their relationship hurts and struggles.

Symbolically, Phyllis envisions herself as the sweet-smelling rose that was birth out of the unknown and unseen struggles of her past, which no one knows what she had experienced to become a rose. For this reason, the rose has become a meaningful symbol found throughout the message she presents to the world.

Currently, Phyllis spends her time as a sought-after holistic (online) relationship consultant, where she keeps it real and raw for her clients as she helps revise their whispers of pain. She is busy teaching and building prophetic prayer warriors and leaders that are Christ conscious, leading by example. Phyllis now resides in Florida with her only child and daughter, Priscilla.

Contact: www.selfwhisper.com and **www.whispervise.org**

"Let this mind be in you which was also in Christ Jesus."

Philippians 2:5